Choosing garden plants

made
easy

Which? Books are commissioned and published by Which? Ltd,
2 Marylebone Road, London NW1 4DF
Email: books@which.co.uk

Distributed by Littlehampton Book Services Ltd,
Faraday Close, Durrington, Worthing, West Sussex BN13 3RB

British Library Cataloguing in Publication Data
A catalogue record for this book is available from the British Library

ISBN 978 1 84490 152 4

1 3 5 7 9 10 8 6 4 2

The publishers would like to thank Ceri Thomas and the *Which? Gardening*
team and Susie Bulman for their help in the preparation of this book.

Consultant editor: Ceri Thomas
Senior editor: Kerenza Swift
Project manager: Emma Callery
Designer: Blanche Williams, Harper Williams Ltd
Proofreader: Sian Stark

Printed and bound by Charterhouse, Hatfield
Distributed by Littlehampton Book Services Ltd, Faraday Close,
Durrington, Worthing, West Sussex BN13 3RB

Essential Velvet is an elemental chlorine-free paper produced at Condat in
Périgord, France using timber from sustainably managed forests. The mill is
ISO14001 and EMAS certified.

For a full list of Which? Books, please call 01903 828557, access our website at
www.which.co.uk/books, or write to Littlehampton Book Services.
For other enquiries call 0800 252 100.

Which?

Choosing garden plants

made easy

Cosmos atrosanguineus 'Chocamocha' (see page 142)

Contents

Introduction

This handy book is a guide to some of the best plants tested and recommended by the *Which? Gardening* experts. *Which? Gardening* has been growing and testing plants since 1984. Each year a selection of popular varieties are grown at test sites around the country, many over two consecutive seasons. The performance of each variety is thoroughly assessed for its qualities, such as shape, resistance to disease, appearance of the flowers and length of flowering. From this extensive and independent testing we have pulled together a selection of our best plants for inclusion in this book.

The book has been arranged by growing condition, to help you select the most appropriate tested plant for a specific condition or place in the garden. Learn how to make the most of your garden, whether you have acid soil, a sunny site, or are keen to plant a flowering border that attracts bees and butterflies. You'll find blazing red *Achillea* 'Feuerland' for coastal sites, popular Oriental poppy 'Patty's Plum' to plant in shade, through to flame-coloured *Zinnia* 'Old Mexico', much loved by bees, and bushy *Clematis* 'Chantilly' – perfect for patio pots.

Each plant entry not only reveals the team's test results and expertise, but also indicates other uses for the plant and is accompanied by an identifying photograph.

Growing symbols

xxxxx soil	Best soil conditions
☀	Grows well in the sun
▮	Grows well in part shade
▦	Grows well in the shade

About the consultant editor
Ceri Thomas

Ceri Thomas is Editor of *Which? Gardening*. She studied horticulture at the University of Reading and RHS Wisley, and is a passionate gardener.

Tulipa 'Irene Parrot' (see page 108)

Tulipa 'Black Jack' (see page 12)

Plants
for spring

Spring is such a magical time as the garden reawakens from its winter rest and plants seem to go whoosh overnight, putting on several inches of growth in a few days. Go away for a weekend and the whole garden will seem to have changed by the time you return, with leaves and flowers unfurling and filling the garden with colour once more.

The secret behind all this growth is the arrival of milder weather and lengthening daylight. Even the birds respond to it by beginning nesting and filling the morning air with their songs. Insects also start to reappear and migrants return to our shores.

Bulbs, such as tulips and daffodils, are perhaps the plants most people associate with this time of year. It's worth taking the time in autumn to buy in new stocks and plant them in borders and containers. Try to buy them as soon as they come in at the garden centre as you'll have the best choice of varieties and you can pick healthy, firm bulbs without any mould. Remember to plant deeply – twice the bulb's depth for narcissus and three times the depth for tulips – and always leave the foliage to die down naturally once the display has finished in spring.

As well as the bulbs, there are many beautiful perennials and shrubs that put on a wonderful display of flowers and new leaves, so include as many as you can for a colourful start to the year.

Tulipa 'Red Hat'

A real stunner. Its velvety flowers are quite unusual with their soft, frilly and fringed edges and dark centres. They drew much admiration from visitors to our trial site. The healthy plants had long, elegant stems and flowered in unison. There's no need to dig up the bulbs after flowering. Instead, remove the dead leaves and mulch with organic matter such as garden compost.

Height: 40cm
Flowering period: April–May
well-drained soil ☀
Also good for: Cut flowers

Tulipa 'Bolroyal Honey'

Originally bred for use as a cut flower, it has all the characteristics you'd expect: the bulbs flower at exactly the same time, hold their shape perfectly and have strong, straight stems. They stood to attention throughout the five weeks they were in flower and showed little sign of spoiling. Don't cut back tulip leaves until they have turned completely brown as while they're still green they are making food to produce next year's displays.

Height: 30cm
Flowering period: April–May
well-drained soil ☀
Also good for: Cut flowers

Tulipa 'Yellow Pomponette'

We've never seen a tulip quite like this one; it looks like an enormous buttercup! The flowers didn't last as long as we'd hoped and it was past its best after a couple of weeks. Tulips are best planted in November when the soil is cool and moist. If you discover some bulbs you haven't planted, don't panic as our trial found that you should still get flowers even if you plant as late as December.

Height: 35cm
Flowering period: April–May
well-drained soil ☀
Also good for: Cut flowers

Tip Squirrels seem to love eating tulip bulbs. We tried all sort of remedies including scattering chilli pepper over the soil. The most effective solution we found was to bury a piece of chicken wire just under the soil surface as it helps stop the squirrels digging up the bulbs.

Tulipa 'Daytona'

With a simple cup-shaped flower, a frilly, frosted fringe and long, elegant stems, this is an attractive and understated tulip that had a touch of class about it. If you garden on heavy soil such as clay, put a layer of horticultural grit or sharp sand at the bottom of the planting hole to help improve drainage and therefore growth.

Height: 40cm
Flowering period: April–May
`well-drained soil` ☀
Also good for: Cut flowers

Tulipa 'Black Jack'

This has to be one of the darkest tulips we've ever seen. Its flowers are typical of cottage types and are about the size of half a tennis ball. The petals have a velvety sheen that you can't resist touching. It was earlier to flower than the established 'Queen of Night' and persisted for five weeks. It has long, straight stems that would be great for cutting and would combine well with white and pink tulips.

Height: 40cm
Flowering period: April–May
`well-drained soil` ☀
Also good for: Cut flowers

Tip Tulips should be planted deeply – three times the depth of the bulb - to give them the best chance of flowering for more than one year. Space the bulbs about 8cm apart.

Narcissus
'Hungarian Rhapsody'

This daffodil proved to be a real eye-catcher in our trial, with its unusual, contrasting split corona. The bulbs flowered in near unison, from the end of March until mid-April, with no flopping or any other notable problems. Plant daffodils to twice their own depth in autumn. For longer-lasting bulbs, plant in fertile, well-drained soil in a sheltered location, away from the strongest winds and worst of the weather.

Height: 40cm
Flowering period: March–April
well-drained soil ☀
Also good for: Cut flowers

Narcissus 'Dickcissel'

Despite its delicate appearance, this daffodil
is surprisingly tough, and it managed
to stay looking great throughout the
inclement weather we experienced during
our trial. With lots of flowering stems and
three blooms on each one, it's not short
of flower power. It has a delicious yet mild
scent, and its bright and breezy flowers are
held gracefully on bowed heads. Buy bulbs
as early as you can for the widest range
and best quality. Buying in larger quantities
and from specialist mail-order suppliers can
give better value for money. Check that
bulbs are firm and show no signs of mould,
and then store them in a cool, dark place
until you plant them.

Height: 30cm
Flowering period: April
`well-drained soil` ☼
Also good for: Scent

Narcissus 'Swoop'

This is the most profusely flowering daffodil
we grew in our trial. From our 23 bulbs we
were graced with more than 80 stems.
The swept-back petals and nodding heads
look great as they flutter gently in the
breeze. When we lifted them, we found
they had been steadily multiplying. Elegant
and prolific, this daffodil would be great
to naturalise around trees and woodland.
Never plant in ground where bulbs have
previously suffered from disease as the
fungal spores can persist in the soil. Lift and
destroy infected bulbs immediately.

Height: 20cm
Flowering period: March–April
`well-drained soil` ☼
Also good for: Naturalising

Hemerocallis dumortieri

The arching, grassy foliage, restrained flower colour and elegant shape made this variety stand out from the crowd, especially when plants came into flower as early as April during our trials, even in Glasgow. The tall stems were covered in long-petaled flowers, which were nicely scented. In the balmy autumn of 2011, our plants produced a second flush of flowers in Glasgow and London. Watch out for hemerocallis gall midge, which can cause buds to swell and then rot. Remove any infected buds if spotted or use a general insecticide.

Height x spread: 80 x 70cm
Flowering period: May, September–October
`well-drained and moist soil` ☀
Also good for: Scent

Centaurea 'John Coutts'

During our trials, *C. hypoleuca* 'John Coutts' flowered in spring and also produced a second flush at all sites bar Beverley. At Glasgow, its second flush was much stronger than the first, and lasted until mid-October. It was much appreciated for its large, fluffy, pink flowers on rain-resistant wiry stems above divided leaves. The flowers are fluffy, vivid lavender-pink with cream centres, measuring 6cm across with dark-brown bract scales. They have large branching stems with coarse grey undersides.

Height x spread: 60 x 60cm
Flowering period: May–July, September–October
`well-drained soil` ☀
Also good for: Bees and butterflies

Hyacinthus 'Madame Sophie'

This unusual hyacinth's unique flowers, with double centres, seemed to bear green flashes while it was opening and gave off a pleasant, subtle scent. The flowers were held on short stout stems and stood bolt upright until after they had faded. Plant hyacinth bulbs 15cm deep and try to put them in groups for the biggest impact from their colourful flowers and scent.

Height: 25cm
Flowering period: March–April
well-drained soil ☀
Also good for: Scent

Luzula sylvatica 'Hohe Tatra'

Greater woodrush is most at home in the shade of a woodland floor, but it proved to be adaptable in our trial and did well, even in full sun. Its tussock of evergreen arching, yellowy-green leaves looked attractive all through the winter, even in the harsh cold of Scotland. By the time the plants had begun to flower, the colour of the new leaves had become more golden yellow and really stood out, even on dull days. Pinky brown sprays of flowers appeared from March and stayed looking good until June. If it is planted in sun, the leaf tips can start to scorch in strong sunlight and should be cut off. Plant with ferns and hostas in some shade for a stunning combination of leaves.

Height x spread: 50 x 50cm
Flowering period: March–June
`well-drained soil`
Also good for: Foliage

Luzula nivea

With its low-key clump of green leaves, this evergreen will sit quietly in your border all year round, but the snowy woodrush lives up to its common name by producing clouds of white flowers in spring. It shows off its charms from May until June or July – often a time when not much else is flowering. Even after the white flowers have finished, the seedheads will carry on looking good for another month or so. It's easy to grow as it doesn't mind sitting in sun or light shade and would really get a chance to shine if combined with the bright colours of perennial oriental poppies.

Height x spread: 50 x 50cm
Flowering period: May–July
`moist soil`
Also good for: Foliage

Ceanothus 'Lemon and Lime'

Intense blue, cone-shaped flower heads appeared in profusion in May and June, complementing the fresh green-and-cream foliage. We got a second, though much smaller, flush of flowers from July to September in our trial. The new leaves, in particular, had very marked variegation, while older leaves turned deeper green. Vigorous plants, ours doubled in size in their first year, but kept to a neat shape, and survived the harsh winter with nothing worse than some brown shoot tips.

Height x spread: 90 x 55cm
Flowering period: May–June
`well-drained soil` ☀
Also good for: Foliage

Corydalis 'Berry Exciting'

The breeders of this plant describe it as: 'A vigorous corydalis with succulent stems and good ferny leaves on a wide-spreading plant.' Our plants soon grew into a low mound of small yellow leaves, covering a large area. The violet flowers, with their dainty spurs, began to open in May. The claims state that the purple flowers are wonderfully fragrant and bloom over a long period of time. We didn't notice any scent, and the colour combination of violet and yellow may not be to everyone's taste, but flowering did go on for months. Our plants seemed unfazed by weeks of drought in early summer, and by the heavy rains that followed. Corydalis self-seeds prolifically; so unwanted seedlings may need removing.

Height x spread: 15 x 25cm
Flowering period: May–July
`moist soil` ▮
Also good for: Containers

Hebe 'Magic Summer'

The breeders of this variety claim: 'Green-and-white leaves with purple-and-red growing tips. Tip colour intensifies in spring and summer.' All plants in our trial kept their purple-and-red colouring at the tips through the year, and any increase in intensity was hard to detect until this spring when 'Magic Summer' did appear slightly darker (it also has slightly larger leaves). Most impressively, they retained their neat shape and colour through a very cold winter, in which many hebes didn't survive, with only a little browning. We also tried these hebes in containers and they looked stunning all through the winter. It's part of a range of four varieties that all have colourful foilage.

Height x spread: 35 x 35cm
Flowering period: all year
well-drained soil ☼
Also good for: Containers

Geum 'Totally Tangerine'

The claims state that the main attributes of this clump-forming plant are robustness, length of flowering season, number of flowers, sterility, vigour and colour. We planted this in July when it was already in flower. Having left it in over winter it began to flower in April, which is around the time you'd expect. Although the name suggests a bad fake tan, the papery petals were delicate shades of pinky apricot. A mass of flowers topped tall sturdy stems that were much less floppy than many geums. A beautiful plant to bridge the gap between spring- and summer-flowering plants.

Height x spread: 60 x 40cm
Flowering period: April–October
well-drained and moist soil ☼ ■
Also good for: Cottage garden borders

Papaver orientale 'Karine' (see page 23)

Plants
for summer

The summer sees most gardens at their peak as plants take advantage of the (hopefully) warm and sunny days. There are plenty of plants to choose from and with careful selection, gardens can look colourful right up to the autumn frosts.

Annuals offer a wide selection of shapes, colours and scents. Hardy varieties, such as poppies and calendula, can be sown in spring directly where you want them to flower, while half-hardy types, such as snapdragons and petunias, can be sown in the greenhouse in spring and then hardened off by gradually introducing them to the outside before planting outdoors once the danger of frost has passed in late May

to early June. If you remove the flowers as they fade, the plants should keep blooming all summer, although hardy annuals tend to burn out earlier than half-hardy ones.

If you don't want to sow seeds, you can either buy plug plants for potting up or full-grown plants in trays. As with annuals, you will find plenty of summer-flowering bulbs, shrubs and perennials in garden centres.

Keep any new plants well watered to help them get through dry spells while they are still putting down roots into the surrounding soil. Mulching around them will help to conserve moisture. Then, towards the end of the summer a feed with tomato food will give them a boost.

Dahlia 'Ivanetti'

A winner with the visitors to our trial site; they loved its dark colour and perfect purple blooms. It outlasted all the other varieties as a cut flower, looking good for at least seven days. But it wasn't the easiest to grow. Growth was rapid and the blooms were heavy, so a storm in June wreaked havoc. It recovered well, but needed careful staking for good results. It's best to set up any support that may be required as early as possible so plants can be tied in as they grow.

Height x spread: 80 x 70cm
Flowering period: July–October
`moist soil` ☀
Also good for: Cut flowers

Papaver orientale 'Lady Frederick Moore'

Big ruffled petals in deep salmon pink top the slender stems of 'Lady Frederick Moore'. The plants in our trial formed bushy clumps, although the foliage was smaller than some varieties. In Glasgow, some plants had to be staked, but in London only one or two stems at the edges flopped outwards – this could be remedied by surrounding with supporting plants. The bright colour faded slightly to whitish pink before the petals dropped but in its full glory it would look spectacular teamed with dark crimson cornflowers (*Centaurea cyanus* 'Black Ball') or the dark purple shoots of *Hebe* 'Amy'.

Height x spread: 80 x 60cm
Flowering period: May–June
`clay and well-drained soil` ☀
Also good for: Cottage garden borders

Papaver orientale 'Karine'

'Karine' is a variety that performed well in our trials. The beautiful flowers have a shallow single layer of pastel pink petals with purple seedheads. Their delicate appearance proved deceptive as the waxy petals held their shape well, even after some very heavy rain. All our plants had masses of flowers during their first flush, and two plants on both sites flowered again later in the summer, though with fewer blooms. They didn't need to be staked. 'Karine' is small enough to be planted at the front of a border with perennial geraniums such as *Geranium clarkei* 'Kashmir Purple'.

Height x spread: 60 x 60cm
Flowering period: May–June,
August–September
`clay and well-drained soil` ☀
Also good for: Cottage garden borders

Kniphofia 'Toffee Nosed'

The classy looking 'Toffee Nosed' earned its name because of its two-tone flowers. It's a relatively new variety that doesn't need a huge amount of room, although the size of our plants did vary. They gave a good show of flowers in the north, but in the warmer, drier south had far more flowers over a much longer time.

Height x spread: 100 x 80cm
Flowering period: July–September
well-drained soil ☀
Also good for: Bees and butterflies

Kniphofia 'Shining Sceptre'

Flowering for weeks and doing almost as well in our Glasgow test site as in north London, the glowing pale orange flowers on bronze stems give a spectacular display of hot colours. Although sold as 'Shining Sceptre', the RHS believe that it is really an older variety called 'Bees' Sunset'. Cut spent flower stems at their base when all the flowers have finished.

Height x spread: 130 x 80cm
Flowering period: June–August
moist and well-drained soil ☀
Also good for: Bees and butterflies

Tip Kniphofias like a sunny spot and deep soil that stays moist in summer. They also need good drainage, so pick a well-drained part of the garden and add organic matter such as garden compost.

Diascia 'Romeo Bright Pink'

With its shockingly bright flowers, this variety stood out as the most vibrantly coloured diascia we grew in our tests. The plants were very neat, initially spreading out almost horizontally then trailing gracefully over the sides of the pot. They were completely covered with flowers, which continued to bloom throughout the summer and into the autumn. As they come from drier climes, diascias don't need massive amounts of water and benefit from good drainage. If plants start to look messy as flowering slows, give them a trim with a pair of shears and some liquid feed. They should flower again in a couple of weeks.

Height x spread: 25 x 30cm, trailing 10cm
Flowering period: June–September
`well-drained soil` :☼:
Also good for: Containers

Cosmos bipinnatus 'Gazebo Red'

In our trials, the simple crimson flowers with their bright yellow centres were really eye-catching, and bees loved them too. The blooms appeared to grow with age, as well as fading slightly in colour. Deadheading was needed at the end of September, but this variety didn't succumb to mildew. 'Gazebo Red' tended to lean over so it would benefit from some support.

Height x spread: 105 x 95cm
Flowering period: July–September
`well-drained soil` :☼:
Also good for: Bees and butterflies

Campanula 'Sarastro'

This is one of the newer varieties and looks set to become a firm favourite. During our trials, stem after stem of fat, deep-purple, waxy flowers opened from dark-purple buds throughout the summer. The stems needed support and in a soggy Glasgow summer the plants were slightly affected by rust, but the flower colour was still good. 'Sarastro' would be best planted in the middle of a border. To help keep the plants looking fresh, lift and divide them every few years.

Height x spread: 80 x 60cm
Flowering period: June–September
moist and well-drained soil ☀ ◼
Also good for: Cottage garden border

Campanula alliariifolia 'Ivory Bells'

This cool and elegant plant needed to be supported in our north London test site, where it was much taller and more floppy than in Glasgow, probably because the soil is more fertile at that test site. The long woody stems were covered along their whole length with small, nodding, white bell-shaped flowers set off nicely by large felty leaves. It didn't spread much, but had a tendency to seed itself around. It would look best in the middle of a border. Most campanulas prefer soil with lime in it (alkaline) and won't cope well in heavy clay. However, many varieties performed well at our Glasgow site, which is on clay. Requirements for sun, shade and moisture aren't very strict, so they're worth trying even if your conditions don't seem ideal.

Height x spread: 80 x 65cm
Flowering period: June–July
moist and well-drained soil ☀ ◼
Also good for: Cottage garden border

Zinnia 'Profusion Cherry'

The Profusion Series has an excellent reputation, and it's not hard to see why. Like other modern hybrids, these were easy to grow in our trial and developed well to form great plants, ideal for bedding. They put on a beautiful display, giving us an abundance of flowers all summer. They showed good resistance to disease and tolerance of poor weather. We also thought their luxuriously rich colour looked great in the garden; as well as red 'Cherry', they're available in orange, yellow and white. Keep plants deadheaded to ensure there is a constant supply of flowers.

Height x spread: 35 x 45cm
Flowering period: June–September
well-drained soil ☼
Also good for: Cut flowers

Agapanthus inapertus 'Midnight Cascade'

In our trials, indigo tubular flowers drooped from the heads, topping elegant stems, in a way typical of the lovely inapertus types. The deep purple colour drew admiring looks from visitors to our trial sites, and our assessors loved it. People with plants that aren't flowering are often advised to be cruel to them by confining them in pots to encourage them to bloom, but the opposite is true. Give them plenty of room and water.

Height x spread: 70 x 60cm
Flowering period: August–September
`well-drained soil` ☀
Also good for: Gravel gardens

Agapanthus Headbourne hybrids

One of the best-known agapanthus varieties, and one that has done well in our trials. Headbourne hybrids gave a fabulous display of lilac-blue flower heads. Agapanthus are often seen growing in pots. While this looks lovely, be aware that it's not ideal for the agapanthus as they'll quickly fill the pots with roots and become hard to water. The best solution is to divide the plant every two years to stop it becoming congested; feed and water in the growing season; and wrap the pot in bubble plastic during winter.

Height x spread: 70 x 75cm
Flowering period: July–August
`well-drained soil` ☀
Also good for: Gravel gardens

Scabiosa japonica 'Ritz Blue'

These were the shortest plants in our trial and, as a result, they were also the neatest. You could use them in a formal bedding scheme without any fear of flopping.

Bees and hoverflies loved them, too. Most scabious plants are blousy rather than tidy, so they fit into cottage-garden plantings better than formal areas. The flowers can be complemented by planting them with other plants of a similar shade.

Height x spread: 25 x 30cm
Flowering period: June–August
well-drained soil ☀
Also good for: Bees and butterflies

Scabiosa atropurpurea 'Fata Morgana'

The lime-green buds turned to pale salmon before opening into soft-yellow blooms with apricot edges. The petals went brown with age, so this one needs deadheading. This a hardy annual type of scabious so you'll need to raise it from seed each spring. We sowed ours in pots of compost in the greenhouse during February and March. We then pricked out the seedlings into individual pots or modules and planted them outside in May.

Height x spread: 85 x 60cm
Flowering period: June–August
well-drained soil ☀
Also good for: Bees and butterflies

Tip Both perennial and annual types of scabious can be raised from seed, but only perennials will return year after year.

Scabiosa 'Summer Berries'

A range of lovely mid pinks, maroon and crimson made 'Summer Berries' one of the best colour mixes in our trial. The shades of the petals meant that, in contrast to many other varieties, any ageing flowers did not become obvious as they started to turn brown. Some deadheading never goes amiss however.

Height x spread: 70 x 65cm
Flowering period: June–August
well-drained soil ☀
Also good for: Bees and butterflies

Scabiosa caucasica 'Perfecta Alba'

This perennial variety stayed more upright than most of the other plants in our trial, despite its height. The milk-white flowers, living up to its name of 'Perfecta Alba' with ragged-edged petals were popular with bees. Scabious do not always germinate easily, so sow plenty of seed to get enough plants. Sow 3mm deep in seed compost. Check the packet for preferred temperatures, some are fussy. We germinated ours in a heated propagator at 20˚C. Prick out seedlings into individual pots or modules and grow on in the greenhouse.

Height x spread: 110 x 55cm
Flowering period: June–August
well-drained soil ☀
Also good for: Bees and butterflies

Scabiosa 'Fire King'

'Fire King' had green buds that turned pink and finally became claret blooms; a unique colour in our trial. The white styles looked a bit like ashes floating out of a fire and the colour combination was enhanced by bright-green leaves. Our members also trialled 'Fire King' and slightly more than half of the respondents said they would grow it again. The flower colour and ease of growing this variety from seed were popular, but one criticism was the overall shape of the plant as they tended to flop over.

Height x spread: 75 x 60cm
Flowering period: June–August
well-drained soil ☀
Also good for: Bees and butterflies

Potentilla 'Volcan'

This plant had the most beautiful flowers in the trial – they were large and double with ruffled petals in a rich, velvety red. They lasted for a respectable 14 weeks and stayed fairly upright. The only other that might have rivalled it was 'Arc-en-ciel', another large-flowered red double we trialled but which didn't make our recommended list. Not all of the 'Arc-en-ciel' plants survived our trial and they didn't have quite as bold a red flower colour – the flowers weren't nearly as abundant as with 'Volcan'. Grow alongside other supporting plants – red or yellow potentillas go well with dahlias, heleniums, ornamental grasses and dark-leafed cannas. Pink potentillas would look lovely with purple sage, meadowsweet (filipendula), agastache and sedum.

Height x spread: 55 x 70cm
Flowering period: July–August
`well-drained soil` ☀
Also good for: Cottage garden border

Veronica gentianoides

Veronica gentianoides is a good mid-border choice, sending up 20cm-long spires of pale blue flowers, embellished with dark blue veins in early summer. These rise well above clumps of handsome, glossy evergreen leaves, which remain fresh after flowering is over. The plant reaches 45cm and likes to be sited on a moist but well-drained soil in full sun or dappled shade and is easy to grow.

Height x spread: 45 x 20cm
Flowering period: May–June
`well-drained soil` ☀ ▮
Also good for: Cut flowers, Cottage garden border

Eremurus 'Joanna'

If it's dramatic height you're after, 'Joanna' is the variety to choose. It was the tallest eremurus in our trial, reaching as high as 230cm in full flower! Everything about 'Joanna' was big, from the sturdy fat stems to the lush foliage. The stems collapsed at our southern site after flowering had finished, but you can cut them down at this stage anyway. Try planting *Allium giganteum* in the same bed and underplant both with hardy geraniums to prolong interest. Eremurus need cold winters to flower well. They are unlikely to thrive in areas with a lot of winter rain as dry winters are essential to prevent rot.

Height x spread: 230 x 10cm
Flowering period: May–June
well-drained soil ☀
Also good for: Scent, Bees and butterflies

Eremurus 'Romance'

The salmony peach colour of 'Romance' was very popular with visitors to our southern trial site in north London. However, flowering was better here in the first year than the second. In the North, 'Romance' was noted as a reliable variety and overall it survived well and flowered for a long time; many of the plants also produced a high number of flowering spikes. Unlike many of the other varieties we grew, 'Romance' stayed upright throughout the trial. Underplant with *Geranium* 'Johnson's Blue', which also thrives in well-drained soil.

Height x spread: 180 x 10cm
Flowering period: May–June
well-drained soil ☀
Also good for: Gravel gardens

Anemone x *hybrida* 'Pretty Lady Emily' (see page 43)

Plants
for autumn

Even with winter on its way, autumn can often feel more like an extension of summer with warm weather and sunshine carrying on as an Indian summer. One sure sign that the seasons are changing, though, are the cooler nights with dew often covering the lawn in the morning. Longer evenings also begin to draw in, keeping us indoors at the end of a busy day instead of in the garden.

Many of the plants we enjoy in autumn actually begin flowering much earlier in the year, but are the real star performers that bloom for months on end, carrying on their display until the first frosts. There's a place for these in any garden as you can't beat them for value for money.

Other plants wait until autumn before they come into their own. Chrysanthemums are perhaps one of the best examples of these plants. They have a reputation as being time-consuming and need careful nurturing in a greenhouse, but in our trial we found lots of great varieties that are hardy enough to stay outdoors and produce masses of flowers. These not only last well in the border but they are also great when cut and brought indoors for the vase.

A good tip is to cut back many varieties by a third in early June as this will make them into branching plants that subsequently need much less staking than if they were left to their own devices.

Dahlia 'Woodside Finale'

In our trials we decided that 'rhubarb and custard' was the most apt way to describe the unusual toning of this dahlia. Our plants grew very fast, so needed to be securely staked early on. They came into their peak in early July, producing lots of small, ball-type flowers. They did well both as a garden plant and as cut flowers, which lasted for at least five days in a vase. For a stunning centrepiece, try putting different varieties of dahlias in a selection of different shapes and colour of vase running down the centre of your dining table.

Height x spread: 115 x 65cm
Flowering period: July–October
`moist soil` ☀
Also good for: Cut flowers

Dahlia 'Oreti Bliss'

A small cactus-type cultivar that's well worth growing as a border plant. Plants romped away with no support and were perpetually smothered with flowers. After deadheading each week, they could be relied on to produce another flush of elegant blooms. They were tough plants and stood up well to bad weather, flowering strongly into October. Try combining this variety with the variegated grass *Miscanthus sinensis* 'Cosmopolitan'.

Height x spread: 105 x 60cm
Flowering period: July–October
`moist soil` ☀
Also good for: Cottage garden border

Tip The striking shapes and colours of dahlias make them fantastic for combining with tropical-looking plants for a jungle-style display.

Dahlia 'Fairfield Frost'

These were a favourite with our assessors. They flowered all summer, producing dozens of delicate blooms. They were a good size and stood up well with only a little support. They needed minimal deadheading and were still flowering profusely in October. The cut flowers lasted for at least four days, but, unlike most other dahlias, weren't very striking in a vase. The white flowers will shine out in twilight, so put 'Fairfield Frost' somewhere you will see it from the patio. You can then savour its blooms as you sit enjoying the evening air. A background of dark-coloured foliage will show it off to its best.

Height x spread: 105 x 60cm
Flowering period: July–October
`moist soil` ☼
Also good for: Cottage garden border

Diascia 'Breezee Apricot'

These were slightly different from many of the other diascias we grew in our trial. They were quite petite and less dense, only trailing slightly. We felt that this demure nature worked in their favour, making them ideal for growing in a rockery or at the front of a border. They were later to start flowering, but they gave us a good show during late summer and were still looking great in mid-October. Diascias prefer a position in full sun and warm conditions for the best flowering. They can be used in pots or baskets, but would be just as happy cascading down a rockery.

Height x spread: 20 x 30cm, trailing 5cm
Flowering period: July–October
`well-drained soil` ☼
Also good for: Containers

Chrysanthemum 'Mei-kyo'

On our trial, the round mounds of our plants were completely covered in hundreds of dainty pink flowers for weeks. There was no sign of white rust and the leaves looked healthy until late in the autumn. 'Mei-kyo' was bushy and didn't need to be cut back or supported. It was small enough that it would look good at the front of a border, and it had a very long flowering season, starting with a brief flush in August, but peaking later in the autumn. The flowers lasted 12 days in a vase.

Height x spread: 50 x 55cm
Flowering period: August-November
moist soil ☀
Also good for: Cut flowers

Chrysanthemum 'Burnt Orange'

This variety isn't widely available yet, but it was so good we felt we had to recommend it. In our trial, though tall, the plants didn't need to be staked even when the flowers were fully out. The grey-green leaves were probably the most attractive in the trial and showed no sign of rust, which can be a problem with chrysanths. The flowers, with spoon-shaped petals, are very distinctive; flowering was late, but the first light frosts didn't stop them looking good.

Height x spread: 115 x 80cm
Flowering period: October–November
moist soil ☀
Also good for: Cut flowers

Chrysanthemum 'Mary Stoker'

Masses of simple but stunningly pretty flowers covered our plants from the end of September, making this a good variety for colder areas. The gorgeous colour changed from apricot to soft pink as the flowers matured. All our plants were healthy and had straight stems, so we didn't need to stake them, but they do need to be pinched or chopped back in June. Cut them back by about a third. This variety lasts two and a half weeks in a vase so is great for cutting.

Height x spread: 90 x 75cm
Flowering period: September–October
moist soil ☀
Also good for: Cut flowers

Tip Chrysanthemums prefer rich soil that retains moisture and need to be planted in a spot in full sun to flower well.

Gladiolus 'Blue Frost'

Pale and interesting, these large frilly flowers are aptly named for their blue-edged white petals. The finished flowers in our trial dropped quite quickly, so didn't look too tatty. None of our plants were staked. Many of the corms produced a couple of flower spikes, with the second often flowering after the first, therefore extending the flowering period. Unless you plan to plant gladioli in large numbers, we would recommend planting them all at the same time and leaving it up to your plants to naturally stagger their own flowering.

Height x spread: 95 x 25cm
Flowering period: September
well-drained soil ☀
Also good for: Cut flowers

Crocosmia x *crocosmiiflora* 'Star of the East'

The seedheads of 'Star of the East' were especially plump, retaining the orange tones of the flowers and ripening to rich mahogany. By autumn, most foliage had died down with the first heavy frost. 'Star of the East' has open stars of golden yellow that fold back on themselves in warm weather. They are generally more tender than other crocosmias. Even in Glasgow, despite a November frost of -8°C and some prolonged frosts in December and January of -6°C, 'Star of the East' survived. Orange crocosmias look good next to plants with broad green leaves, such as cannas, or purple foliage, like *Eucomis comosa* 'Sparkling Burgundy' or *Cotinus* 'Grace'.

Height x spread: 70 x 10cm
Flowering period: August–October
well-drained soil ☀
Also good for: Foliage

Veronica spicata 'Rotfuchs'

In our trials, *V. spicata* 'Rotfuchs' (which is also sold as 'Red Fox') came into flower from late June or July, with its deep pinkish-red spikes. Its flowers and dense foliage were appreciated, but it was rather too short to show these off to best advantage. At Glasgow, its strong colour and abundance of flowers put it among the top performers. Veronicas prefer full sun. The shorter carpeters and clump-formers are best at the front of borders, but once flowering is over, the foliage can look tired, so position the plants carefully to avoid a hole appearing in your border.

Height x spread: 40 x 30cm
Flowering period: July–September
well-drained and moist soil ☀
Also good for: Cottage garden border

Fothergilla x *intermedia* 'Blue Shadow'

'Blue Shadow' has white flowers in spring, powder-blue grey foliage in summer and a mix of rich-red, orange and yellow leaf colours in autumn. Fothergilla is an unusual deciduous shrub, with a leaf colour similar to eucalyptus. The creamy white bottlebrush flowers were almost over when we planted ours in late May (they open before it comes into leaf), but we loved the verdigris blue leaves that covered caramel stems. The range of leaf colours in autumn was just as described and it would be worth growing for those alone. Fothergilla is an acid-loving plant, but performed well in our neutral soil.

Height x spread: 150 x 150cm
Flowering period: all year
acid soil ☀ ◼
Also good for: Containers, Foliage

Carex buchananii 'Green Twist'

A seed strain of *Carex buchananii*, 'Green Twist' has light olive-green, upright foliage that twists slightly at the tips. With its slim clumps of upright leaves and curly tips, we thought that 'Green Twist' was a very decorative plant. Its subtle olive colour makes it an excellent companion for more showy plants, and it would work very well in a pot because it's quite compact. This carex really came into its own as a winter foliage plant, when the curly tips were one of the few things looking pretty outside in the frost and snow.

Height x spread: 50 x 30cm
Flowering period: May–October
well-drained soil ☀
Also good for: Containers, Foliage

Mahonia nitens 'Cabaret'

The breeders of this plant claim: 'An amazing new colour introduction to the mahonia range. Glossy foliage and unique orange-red flower buds open yellow from September through autumn.' With short flower spikes covered in red buds, that open into beautiful butter-yellow flowers, we found this to be a striking shrub in autumn. Unlike most mahonias it doesn't flower into winter; the long, shiny evergreen foliage kept it attractive then, though. Once open, the flowers didn't last long and they didn't seem to have the delicious scent of other mahonias. Plants should reach 65 x 50cm, maximum, so would fit into a smaller space than other varieties.

Height x spread: 65 x 50cm
Flowering period: September–October
well-drained soil ▮
Also good for: Foliage

Anemone x *hybrida* 'Pretty Lady Emily'

Our Japanese anemones, planted in June, weren't particularly early to come into flower, with the buds opening in September. The large, double flowers were softly pink-coloured. They flowered well into October, though, and were much shorter than most Japanese anemones, with flower stems growing to about 15cm above the tops of the green leaves. The sugar-pink, double flowers were plentiful and as big as you'd expect to get on a larger plant. We also grew 'Pretty Lady Julia' (large, single, light-pink flowers) and 'Pretty Lady Susan' (single, darker rose-pink flowers), which flowered around the same time and were also compact.

Height x spread: 40 x 35cm
Flowering period: September–October
well-drained and moist soil
Also good for: Containers

Caryopteris x *clandonensis* 'Sterling Silver'

The plant breeders claim: 'Shimmering soft-silver foliage throughout summer, topped with intense blue flowers in September to October.' These neat little shrubs had very pale, silvery-green leaves, which graced the upright stems from spring to early summer. The intense indigo-blue of the flowers made for a striking contrast and was a bonus at the end of the summer. Our plants were only in flower for a couple of weeks in their first year, but they should bloom for longer when established, and were well worth growing for the lovely leaves alone.

Height x spread: 30 x 30cm
Flowering period: September
well-drained soil
Also good for: Foliage, Gravel gardens

Echinacea purpurea 'Kim's Mop Head' (see page 49)

Plants
for winter

Winter sees most of us tucked up indoors instead of out in the garden. Rather than fight this natural instinct, it's best to design your garden around it by keeping the winter colour near to the house so that you can enjoy it by looking out of the window.

For a warm welcome home, make sure you have containers planted with winter colour near the front door. Pansies and violas are a great choice for reliable flowers through all but the coldest weather. Cyclamen and ornamental cabbage add striking colour, but make sure you shelter them from winter wet or they will rot off.

Colourful foliage is also a must. Variegated ivies, sedge and euonymus are just a few of the things you could choose from. They can all be planted out in the garden after winter is over when you dismantle the container.

There are some plants that choose to flower at this time of year, including the heavily scented shrub *Viburnum* x *bodnantense* 'Dawn', yellow-flowered winter jasmine (*Jasminum nudiflorum*) and, of course, snowdrops. These are all an absolute joy in a garden that is otherwise at rest.

Not all flowers have to be fresh to look good in winter, though, as there are plenty of types that remain looking striking, even after they turn brown and die. Look for ones with strong outlines, such as sea holly and echinacea, as these look particularly good when sprinkled with frost.

Sedum 'Matrona'

Statuesque and colourful, this sedum has pinky tints and purple veins in the leaves and stems, which set off its pink star-shaped flowers beautifully. It held its shape well in our tests, so wouldn't need to be cut back. Like some other varieties of sedum, 'Matrona' benefits from a Chelsea chop. This involves cutting the stems back by up to half at the end of May to encourage plants to become more bushy. The flowers fade by winter, but they continue to look good even when they have turned brown, especially on a frosty morning.

Height x spread: 65 x 85cm
Flowering period: July–September
well-drained soil ☀
Also good for: Foliage, Bees and butterflies

Sedum 'Mr Goodbud'

If your borders need a shot of vibrant colour in late summer, you should try this lovely sedum, with its bright pink and purple flowers. The leaves of our plants were purple-edged and the strong, upright stems tinted pink, adding further to its colourful impact. The flowers look good in winter, even though they'll be dead and brown, as they have such a structural outline that looks wonderful when covered in frost.

Height x spread: 50 x 70cm
Flowering period: August–October
well-drained soil ☀
Also good for: Bees and butterflies

Tip Cut back the stems of sedum to ground level in January to allow the new green shoots to push through the soil.

Allium 'Beau Regard'

The round, silvery-purple flower heads were a sight for sore eyes in our trial. Individual, star-shaped flowers were packed tightly into large spheres and held in exceptional uniformity on the tall, bare stems to give an outstanding display. At our southern trial site we had flowers from late April that held their colour until mid-June. Flowering was slightly later in Scotland, beginning in mid-May. But even when the colour had faded from the flowers, the seedheads remained attractive and intact atop the strong stems. They fade to an attractive biscuit-brown by winter and look like a ball of little stars. The stems will eventually fall over; when they do, cut them back to ground level.

Height x spread: 100 x 60cm
Flowering period: late April–mid-June
`well-drained soil` ☼
Also good for: Bees and butterflies

Viola 'Endurio Pink Shades' and 'Endurio Mixed'

The claims state that this viola is semi-trailing and will flower through the winter. We grew 'Endurio Pink Shades' from plants, and mixed colours of 'Endurio' from seed. 'Pink Shades' were in flower in November and bloomed non-stop through the winter, including during a week of snow. Plants raised from seed in late summer flowered in spring. They all had a delicious sweet scent. Our plants suffered from some fungal leaf spots in spring that became severe, but they recovered to reflower well in May and June.

Height x spread: 30 x 25cm
Flowering period: November–February, April–June
`well-drained soil` ☼
Also good for: Containers

Ferula communis

In our trials, this giant fennel had large, very dark green curly filigree foliage which looked good all through the winter in the warmer locations of Dorset and London, though less so in Scotland. In the summer it died down when the weather warmed up, but reappeared later in the season. It can produce a tall flower spike, but didn't on most of our plants. Try planting this in a hot, dry part of the garden. The sculptural flower spikes continue to look good even when dead in winter.

Height x spread: 3 x 1m
Flowering period: July–August
well-drained soil
Also good for: Gravel gardens

Echinacea purpurea 'Kim's Mop Head'

In our trials, the simple and elegant, 'Kim's Mop Head' had white petals that started life as a horizontal fringe around the green and orange cone and then dropped downwards as the flower matured. It was a sturdy plant with strong, self-supporting flower stems that did well everywhere except on the heavy soil in our Glasgow site. The flowers brightened up some very dull days and would look good with New Zealand Iris (*Libertia peregrinans*), whose leaves would echo the orange and green of the echinacea's cones. Leave on the dead flowers as the cones look dramatic in winter.

Height x spread: 70 x 50cm
Flowering period: July–September
moist and well-drained soil
Also good for: Cottage garden border

Euphorbia x *martini* 'Ascot Rainbow'

The plant breeder claims that: 'This euphorbia has distinct and unique variegated foliage in tones of cream, green-blue and red-pink when colder. The flowers are cream, lime, green and white.' With chubby rosettes of yellow and blue-green variegated leaves, this evergreen euphorbia looked good throughout summer in our trials. The top leaves started to turn an attractive pink and red as the temperature cooled and it produced large clusters of cream and green flowers.

Height x spread: 35 x 40cm
Flowering period: May–June
well-drained and dry soil
Also good for: Gravel gardens

Crocosmia 'Severn Sunrise'

Vibrant glowing buds of flame red, burnished orange or warm yellow erupt from slender leaves in late summer. 'Severn Sunrise' was much admired in our trials for its mass of small flowers that fade to an unusual pink. By autumn, most foliage had died down with the first heavy frost, but the leaves remained all winter in north London. Its tight, upright clump of leaves, with statuesque seedheads, made it more attractive than some that still had late flowers. The striking outline continues to look good into early to mid-winter.

Height x spread: 100 x 50cm
Flowering period: August–September
well-drained soil ☀
Also good for: Foliage

Viöla 'Pot Pourri Mixed'

These colourful beauties will carpet beds and containers with hundreds of blooms throughout late winter and spring. With bobbing heads in a variety of yellows, mauves and white, this pretty mix of violas flowered their socks off in our trial. We planted them, already in flower, in early July. With deadheading and a light trim, they bloomed into November, took a breather during the coldest months, then began flowering again in January and were still in flower in June. The claims state that each fragrance of Viola 'Pot Pourri Mixed' can be identified, from fresh spring blooms to citrus and honey. We had to get quite close to smell the scent, which was fresh but faint.

Height x spread: 25 x 35cm
Flowering period: July–November, January–June
well-drained soil ☀ ■
Also good for: Containers

Viola 'Sorbet Mixed'

The sheer vivacity of this viola mix in autumn, early winter and spring makes up for its limited display in January and February. This is a bushy and compact variety and would look equally good in container displays or at the front of borders. We found that the colours gelled well together.

Height x spread: 25 x 20cm
Flowering period: October–May
well-drained soil
Also good for: Containers

Anemone x *hybrida*
'Honorine Jobert' (see page 57)

Plants
for clay soil

Clay soil is not the nightmare that many books would have you believe. It's true that it does hold moisture when it rains and then cracks in dry weather, but these cracks are what drains the soil so they are not necessarily bad news. Clay also holds on to nutrients well so plants are generally healthy and lush.

When you first tackle a garden with clay soil it's worth putting in a bit of effort and digging it well. Many people fear treading on clay when it's wet as they don't want to compact it. Clay compacts naturally, however, so it is worth taking the risk and digging in wetter conditions than you might like, than not doing it at all. Hold the spade so that the blade is at a right angle to the soil and use your weight to drive it right in. The angle between the handle and the blade is designed to make your job easier, but to do its job, it needs this right angle. The first spadeful will be difficult to turn, but it gets easier.

Order a load of cheap unwashed sand (quarrymen often discard the top layers from the quarry) and slowly spread it over the dug surface. A depth of 5cm is ideal, then dress with organic material, such as garden compost or well-rotted manure.

The worms will do the work of mixing and the effect is persistent and magical. In subsequent years, put organic material on the surface, but never dig it in.

Clay soil

Astrantia 'Hadspen Blood'

'Hadspen Blood' has a vigorous green mound of foliage nearer the flowers, which helps to offset these richly coloured deep red blooms. We found many astrantias flowered non-stop from May until October if regularly deadheaded; there were always new flowering shoots coming up to take their place. Cutting back all the old flowering stems rejuvenates the plants for their second flowering. Subsequent flowers were often just as good as the first, but with a bigger mound of foliage by this time, and just as popular with butterflies and bees.

Height x spread: 75 x 60cm
Flowering period: May–October
`clay soil` ☀
Also good for: Foliage, Bees and butterflies

Astrantia major 'Alba'

We found 'Alba' opened as a greenish-white flower that looked dirty from a distance. But from August onwards it became a clear white that really shone out in the autumn months. We found many astrantias flowered non-stop from May until October if regularly deadheaded; there were always new flowering shoots coming up to take their place. Cutting back all the old flowering stems rejuvenates the plants for their second flowering. Subsequent flowers were often just as good as the first, but with a bigger mound of foliage by this time, and just as popular with butterflies and bees. Despite heavy rain, none needed staking once established and the flowers were unblemished by the weather.

Height x spread: 80 x 45cm
Flowering period: June–October
`clay soil` ☀
Also good for: Bees and butterflies

Hosta 'Queen Josephine'

Glossy green centres flow into creamy-yellow edging on this hosta's leaves. This, plus the deep ribbing and graceful heart shape, helped make them some of the most attractive in the trial. The plants flowered freely, too, with mauve/lilac blooms. At our London trial garden, the plants suffered from the fungal disease rust, largely because they were struggling with too much sun and the drier conditions. Plants had no such trouble in Glasgow, flowering from mid-June to August, but they did suffer quite a bit of slug and snail damage on a couple of the plants, while the rust-troubled London ones were largely left alone.

Height x spread: 25 x 40cm
Flowering period: July–August
`clay soil`
Also good for: Well-drained soil, Moist soil, Foliage, Summer flowers

Hosta 'Praying Hands'

'Praying Hands' gets its name from its upright stems and slender folded leaves, which look like hands clasped in prayer. It is also thought that the shape makes it less liable to damage by slugs and snails, as the leaves are held well away from the soil. The slugs and snails found their way to them in our trial, though, and there was some damage on all the plants. At our London site, plants also struggled with the drier conditions and never formed much of a clump. They did better at Glasgow, where they flowered well and were described as 'elegant and distinguished' by our assessors.

Height x spread: 80 x 60cm
Flowering period: May–June
`clay soil`
Also good for: Well-drained soil, Moist soil, Foliage, Summer flowers

Papaver orientale 'Turkish Delight'

The exceptionally beautiful pale pink flowers of 'Turkish Delight' made it a strong favourite in our trial gardens. There were no markings on the petals but the frothy mass of purple stamens around the seed pod made a fantastic contrast to the mouth-watering pink of the crinkled petals. The stems stood up well in wet and windy conditions but only one plant re-flowered on both test sites. Try planting it with the ornamental millet *Pennisetum glaucum* 'Purple Majesty', which has dramatic purple leaves and can be easily grown from seed. Cut the plant to the ground once it finishes flowering and it will resprout with a clump of fresh new leaves.

Height x spread: 80 x 60cm
Flowering period: May–June
clay soil ☀
Also good for: Well-drained soil

Anemone x *hybrida* 'Honorine Jobert'

Tough and winter hardy, these stalwart late-flowering plants form thick clumps of handsome leaves and strong stems carrying single white blooms. 'Honorine Jobert' was the best white variety we grew in our trial, flowering for 5–8 weeks. This variety reached 100cm in height.

Height x spread: 100 x 75cm
Flowering period: September–November
clay soil :☀:
Also good for: Moist soil

Coreopsis 'Limerock Dream'

This tender herbaceous perennial has pinky-orange flowers all summer on neat mounds of foliage. In our trial, it produced a sea of unusually coloured copper-pink flowers. It flowered in two main flushes (July and September) and was very popular with bees and hoverflies. The plants didn't flop and survived the winter well in north London. A great addition to the front or middle of a border. The plant is said to be very drought tolerant.

Height x spread: 55 x 90cm
Flowering period: July–October
clay soil :☀:
Also good for: Bees and butterflies

> **Tip** Oriental poppies can look messy when they finish flowering as the plant collapses. The best solution is to cut the stems back to ground level as soon as the flowers finish. You may even get some late-season blooms.

Crocosmia 'Spitfire'

'Spitfire' was floriferous and bright in our tests, but the spent flowers have a tendency to remain on the heads untidily so cut back the flowering stems at the base once they've finished. This variety has brilliant orange-red, upward-facing flowers.

Height x spread: 75 x 45cm
Flowering period: July–August
clay soil ☀
Also good for: Moist soil, Well-drained soil, Foliage

> **Tip** Crocosmias can make large, congested clumps if left to their own devices. Keep yours full of vigour by lifting the clump every few years between November and June. Pull apart into smaller clumps and replant.

Crocosmia 'Lucifer'

This plant is a scorcher – not just because of its flaming trumpet blooms, but also for its sheer flower power. Once it gets established you can expect a dazzling show of flowers that last for several months. It soon forms a large clump but isn't invasive. Some varieties have bronze and stiffly pleated foliage, providing additional architectural value from early summer until September. These jewels of southern Africa shoot from underground corms, but are best bought as actively growing perennials. Their seedheads are rather attractive, too. Its bright colour makes it useful for dropping in among other plants to liven up a border.

Height x spread: 120 x 100cm
Flowering period: July–September
clay soil ☀
Also good for: Moist soil, Well-drained soil, Foliage

Helenium 'Moerheim Beauty'

High summer wouldn't be the same without cheery daisies. The most impressive are the heleniums with many reliable varieties. For the most vivid colour choose 'Moerheim Beauty', with 130cm-tall blooms ranging from tan-yellow to rusty-red. The blooms darken as they age. All have an upright, branching habit and flower freely from July to September, for around 10 weeks. 'Moerheim Beauty' stood up to very heavy rain at our Glasgow site without staking. The plant does well in clay but prefers soil that has been improved by adding sand and organic matter.

Height x spread: 130 x 40cm
Flowering period: July–September
`clay soil` :☀:
Also good for: Cut flowers, Bees and butterflies

Leucanthemum x *superbum* 'Bishopstone'

With its eccentric, feathery flowers, this is a charming plant. It flowers freely for around eight weeks and forms a neat mound of colour. It's a good choice if you like cut flowers as they last well in a vase, and you'll be able to enjoy plenty of them. They are very easy to grow. 'Bishopstone' can also be grown in partial shade. Try combining it in the border with phlox or some striking ornamental grasses.

Height x spread: 90 x 60cm
Flowering period: July–August
`clay soil` :☀:
Also good for: Moist soil, Well-drained soil, Cut flowers

Potentilla atrosanguinea var. argyrophylla (see page 66)

Plants
for well-drained soil

Well-drained soils tend to be either sandy or stony and hence dry. Don't fight the lack of moisture in well-drained soil by watering all the time, but revel in its extraordinary advantages. You can grow all kinds of wonderful, colourful and scented plants that people who are less favoured will either struggle or be unable to grow. Think of Mediterranean plants with scented foliage and beautiful flowers, and many more. There's a huge list of plants that will thrive. Some lucky gardeners enjoy moist but well-drained soil, so the list of plants they can grow is even broader.

Our trial grounds at Capel Manor in north London have well-drained soil, which we've improved over the years by digging in organic matter such as well-rotted manure or garden compost, and also by covering the surface with a layer of mulch each year.

Planting and establishing need attention. Water plants thoroughly before planting – leave them in a bucket of water until the compost is dark and moist. Planting in autumn, winter or early spring is better because there is more moisture available (and the water demanded by growing plants is less). However, when the tops begin to grow in later spring, give water until the plant is established. Mulching around plants will also help to conserve whatever moisture there is in the ground so it's available for the plants to use.

Salvia nemorosa 'Pink Friesland'

This herbaceous perennial has pink flowers all summer. It tolerates dry conditions when established. In our tests, this plant was a haze of mauve all summer, thanks to its purple flower spikes and pink flowers – and there were bees buzzing all over them. The aromatic foliage formed neat mounds. It was troubled by fungal disease in its first winter but it quickly recovered. Cut back after flowering to keep tidy.

Height x spread: 55 x 90cm
Flowering period: June–August
well-drained soil
Also good for: Bees and butterflies

Kniphofia 'Tawny King'

If you like the dynamic shape of kniphofia but aren't so keen on the very hot colours, 'Tawny King' would be a good compromise. The tall stems weren't produced in very large numbers in our trial, but the narrow flower heads lasted really well. The plant is vigorous and easy to grow. The stems are dark bronze in colour which contrasts beautifully with the cream flowers. They were in bloom for longer than any other variety we trialled in Glasgow and longer than most in our north London site.

Height x spread: 130 x 70cm
Flowering period: July–September
well-drained soil ☀
Also good for: Bees and butterflies

Kniphofia 'Fiery Fred'

'Fiery Fred', which is named after cricketer Fred Trueman, gave a spectacular display of flaming colour for weeks in both our Glasgow and north London test sites. The long, sturdy flower stems were plentiful and the clumps are a manageable size for most gardens. If you'd like a bit of drama in your garden but don't have huge borders, this would certainly fit the bill. Leave the old leaves on the plants over winter. Cut them back as new growth starts in spring. Old clumps can be divided in late winter while they are dormant

Height x spread: 130 x 80cm
Flowering period: June–August
moist and well-drained soil ☀
Also good for: Bees and butterflies

Tip Kniphofia don't like very cold or very wet winters. Mulch with a 5–8cm layer of well-rotted, organic matter in late autumn to help protect them during winter.

Papaver 'Bright Star'

The extraordinary colour of the blooms in the Super Poppy Series was described by one of our Scottish assessors as 'luxurious deep raspberry red' with pleated petals that looked 'like scrunched tissue'. At our London test site, our assessors noticed a bluish hue to the red, and everyone agreed they looked fantastic. 'Bright Star' produced masses of flowers in May–June and a second, smaller, flush of blooms on both the London and Glasgow sites in August–September. The only drawback was that despite the claims made for Super Poppy Series, this variety needed to be staked or plants flopped quite badly. But the unusual colour gave a modern twist to a traditional plant, and 'Bright Star' could be used as a vivid contrast to cardoons (*Cynara cardunculus*) or blue grasses such as blue oat grass (*Helictotrichon sempervirens*) or *Festuca glauca*.

Height x spread: 80 x 70cm
Flowering period: May–June,
August–September
Clay and well-drained soil ☀
Also good for: Summer flowers

Zinnia 'Aztec Sunset'

The plants spread well in our tests, with short stems that bore masses of small single and double flowers. Their vibrant blooms in a mix of 'hot' colours would look great in a tropical-style planting. They were tough little plants that flowered persistently, and it took a long time before powdery mildew had any effect on them.

Height x spread: 45 x 50cm
Flowering period: mid-July–September
well-drained soil ☀
Also good for: Cut flowers

Eremurus 'Jeanne-Claire'

In our tests, 'Jeanne-Claire' produced lots of flowering spikes per plant, but this variety also excelled in length of flowering time. The lemon-yellow flowers were gathered into tall but slim spikes. As with many eremurus, its leaves aren't very attractive after flowering, so underplant them with something like *Euphorbia characias* subsp. *wulfenii*, which thrives in similar soil, has lime-green flowers and blue-green leaves. Eremurus need cold winters to flower well, although dry winters are essential to prevent rot. Place them in a bed with rich, free-draining soil. Choose a sheltered place protected from wind but make sure it's not shady as they need sunshine too.

Height: 175cm
Flowering period: June–July
well-drained soil ☀
Also good for: Gravel gardens

Eremurus x *isabellinus* Ruiter hybrids

E. x *isabellinus* Ruiter hybrids was the only variety in which every plant in the trial produced a flowering spike in both years. It also flowered for the longest time, producing spikes with separate colours ranging from white through apricot, egg yolk yellow and pink to orange. We noticed the heights varied from colour to colour, so they weren't very uniform. Perhaps because of their long flowering period, Ruiter hybrids suffered more from blackfly than other varieties. Try a carpet of *Allium karataviense* beneath for some ground cover.

Height: 155cm
Flowering period: June–July
well-drained soil ☀
Also good for: Gravel gardens

Potentilla atrosanguinea var. *argyrophylla*

Everyone who trialled this plant at our five test sites loved the ochre colour of the flowers, which contrasted so well with the silvery leaves. It did tend to sprawl – with the flowers being produced on long stems away from the main clump of foliage – but it would make good ground cover. This plant did moderately well in its first year, but by the time it had settled in, it was recommended at all the test sites. Position at the front of the border. Grow alongside other supporting plants – red or yellow potentillas go well with dahlias, heleniums, ornamental grasses and dark-leafed cannas. Cut stems back to ground level in spring. They are generally pest and disease free.

Height x spread: 40 x 95cm
Flowering period: June–July
well-drained soil :☀:
Also good for: Cottage garden borders

Potentilla x *hopwoodiana*

It was the sheer flower power of this vigorous plant that made it stand out from the crowd. The pale pink and cream blooms smothered the plants and stood out against the green foliage. The flower stems did sprawl a bit during our trials, but the flowers were so attractive and prolific that it would still make a wonderful addition to a cottage garden. Use it to soften the edges of paths and borders or grow it among other plants that can support the stems. Position and cut back as for *Potentilla atrosanguinea* var. *argyrophylla* (above).

Height x spread: 45 x 75cm
Flowering period: July–October
well-drained soil :☀:
Also good for: Cottage garden borders

Gladiolus 'Tinkerbelle'

The lovely thing about these medium-sized, pale-orange flowers is the red streaking at the edges of the petals, which, when seen from a distance, turns the colour to burnt orange. The clumps of foliage are quite narrow, so you may need to plant this variety a little closer together than others. The plants in our trial were a bit floppy; most of them needed staking. But it was worth the effort.

Height x spread: 120 x 20cm
Flowering period: August
well-drained soil ☀
Also good for: Foliage

Well-drained soil

Cosmos bipinnatus 'Sweet Sixteen'

The flowers of 'Sweet Sixteen' varied a lot in our trials – some were white with a pink edge, others were pink with a darker edge and some were fully crimson. Some had a central 'ruff' of mini petals around the eye and others didn't! They were all very pretty, though. The flowers were quite small but there were lots of them, and they were a magnet for bumblebees, honeybees and hoverflies. This variety also makes a great cut flower. The plants were big (up to 116cm tall) with lots of dense, feathery leaves. Not surprisingly, some of the plants at the edge of the plot tended to lean over, so they'd benefit from staking.

Height x spread: 115 x 110cm
Flowering period: July–September
`well-drained soil` ☀
Also good for: Bees and butterflies

Hosta 'Blue Mouse Ears'

This was an irresistible little plant, so small that it's probably best suited to planting in a pot rather than a bed. In our tests, the blue spoon-shaped leaves did indeed look like the ears of a mouse. Smaller hostas tend to have less vigorous roots and often do better on lighter soil,. There was almost no slug damage to those in London, though there were a few holes in Glasgow. 'Blue Mouse Ears' could be grown as a specimen in a small pot with a coloured gravel mulch, or plant them in a lightly shaded part of a rock garden with some thrift, alpine campanulas and *Dianthus deltoides*.

Height x spread: 10 x 25cm
Flowering period: June–July
`well-drained soil` ☀ ▮
Also good for: Foliage, Containers

Echinacea purpurea 'Ruby Giant'

With its heavy clay soil that stays wet in winter, the Glasgow trial site proved the trickiest place to grow coneflowers, but 'Ruby Giant' came up trumps as one of only four varieties that grew well there. Giant in terms of its height and flower size, this was a favourite with all our assessors. They liked its huge orange cones and deep pink petals, its sweet scent and sheer number of flowers. It was a bit floppy, but could be supported by surrounding plants such as purple moor grass (*Molinia caerulea* subsp. *arundinacea* 'Variegata').

Height x spread: 80 x 60cm
Flowering period: July–September
Clay and well-drained soil ☀
Also good for: Scent

Helictotrichon sempervirens

Blue oat grass is a real beauty from the Mediterranean with its clumps of tall, silvery-blue and needle-thin leaves. Gracefully arching flower stalks appear during April and May, and at first these match the blue colour of the leaves, later turning a pale biscuit colour. Flowers only need to be removed when they flop towards the end of the season. Blue oat grass stayed evergreen throughout winter in our trial, except for Scotland where the foliage died down for a couple of months. Run your fingers through the plants to remove any dead leaves. Plant where the sun can shine through the flowers and surround with dusky pink tulips for a striking contrast.

Height x spread: 120 x 70cm
Flowering period: April–May
well-drained soil ☀
Also good for: Foliage

Helleborus 'Pink Beauty' (see page 75)

Plants
for chalky soil

The classic sign that you're growing on a chalky soil is lumps of white chalk in the soil, but not all alkaline soils contain chalk. If you're not sure whether your soil is alkaline, buy a simple soil-test kit from the garden centre (pH7 to 8.5 are alkaline, above 8.5 is rare in the UK) or see if your neighbours are growing lime-haters such as rhododendrons and camellias.

The majority of garden plants cope well with alkalinity. So, as it's not easy to reduce soil pH and make it more acidic, go with the swim and plant whatever you fancy. Be aware, too, that a plant's response to alkaline soil is not all or nothing. Some day lilies, for example, thrive at pH7.5,

but take five years to die at 8.5. Other day lilies will happily grow at 8.5.

It's not only the pH of chalky soils that can prove challenging as they are often shallow, stony and free-draining. This means that plants are vulnerable to drought. Organic matter, such as garden compost, decomposes rapidly, so you may need to use fertilisers to keep your plants growing strongly. Mulching regularly with organic matter will also help as it conserves moisture in the soil. If you're planting shrubs and trees, you may need to break up the sub-soil as it's often in a hard layer, which makes it difficult to dig a deep enough planting hole.

Aster amellus 'Violet Queen'

'Violet Queen' has the most compelling violet flowers. At four test sites, it grew to 50–65cm, flowered from September to November and lasted 10 weeks in Leeds. It flowers in late summer and autumn like other michaelmas daisies, but it has no running propensities and is a compact height. The petals are an intense deep violet with greenish-yellow centres. It is also sold as 'Veilchenkonigin'.

Height x spread: 65 x 25cm
Flowering period: September–November
chalky soil ☀
Also good for: Well-drained soil

Aster x *frikartii* 'Mönch'

Aster x *frikartii* 'Mönch' was truly outstanding when we trialled it, flowering for at least seven weeks at our five regional test sites and for 11 weeks at three of them. In our trial it began flowering in August, but it's been known to bloom as early as June. Unlike many michelmas daisies it doesn't suffer from powdery mildew. Its classic planting partner is the yellow, black-eyed rudbeckia daisy.

Height x spread: 90 x 40cm
Flowering period: September–October
chalky soil ☀
Also good for: Well-drained soil

Echinops ritro

Few plants are more effective at giving your borders texture than thistles, with their spiky blooms, stems and leaves. There are few true thistles you'd want to invite into your garden, but of the perennial lookalikes, echinops, or globe thistle, is one of the best. It's a coarse, branching plant with grey-green foliage and blue spiky, rounded blooms. We find the most free-flowering species is *E. ritro*, which also gives the longest display of 5cm orbs in July to August. By the end of the season it can become quite large, 170 x 80cm, and also scruffy at the base, so is best planted near the back of the border. We also recommend *E. ritro* subsp. *ruthenicus*. This is a paler but later choice that flowers with aplomb from August to September.

Height x spread: 170 x 80cm
Flowering period: July–August
chalky soil ☀
Also good for: Well-drained soil

Achillea millefolium 'Rose Madder'

The vibrant pink blooms of 'Rose Madder' caught everyone's attention at our test sites. They appeared later than most of the other achilleas, in late June. The numerous flowers were still attractive later in the year and kept a pale rose-pink colour. Although this is one of the smaller achilleas, it required staking. Nevertheless, the stunning flower colour and long flowering period make this plant worth the effort. Deadhead regularly and divide in autumn or spring every three years. Achillea leaves can aggravate skin conditions.

Height x spread: 60 x 70cm
Flowering period: June–September
`chalky and well-drained soil` ☀
Also good for: Coastal

Achillea 'Moonshine'

Although this achillea has soft yellow flowers, it nevertheless makes a tremendous impact – always the first to come out and flowering for an average of 19 weeks between May and October. Its feathery, silver-green foliage set off the yellow flowers really well in our trials. This would be a great choice for a smaller garden as it only reaches 60cm tall.

Height x spread: 60 x 75cm
Flowering period: May–October
`chalky and well-drained soil` ☀
Also good for: Coastal

Tip For sturdy, vigorous achillea plants and a long flowering period, deadhead blooms regularly and divide in autumn or spring every three years.

Helleborus argutifolius 'Silver Lace'

This free-flowering hellebore had masses of pinkish-green blooms in spring during our trial. The flowers were large and outward-facing so gave lots of impact in the bleak winter months. The leaves have a beautiful pewtered colouring with green veins. They were set off well by the glossy, evergreen foliage, which formed neat clumps in our trial beds. Thin the leaves after flowering to keep plants healthy. Cut off the old flower stems as they fade to make way for the new leaves that are bursting through. It's a good plant for gardens that are visited by deers as it is said to be less palatable to them.

Height x spread: 50 x 45cm
Flowering period: February–April
chalky and well-drained soil
Also good for: Foliage

Helleborus 'Pink Beauty'

This free-flowering hellebore was absolutely covered with blooms in spring. The flowers are ivory-pink and open from pink buds. They then age to a beautiful dusky pink. In our trials, the flowers were large and outward-facing so gave lots of impact in the bleak winter months. They were set off well by the glossy, evergreen foliage mottled with silver, which formed neat clumps in our trial beds. As with 'Silver Lace' (above), thin the leaves after flowering to keep plants healthy.

Height x spread: 50 x 45cm
Flowering period: February–April
chalky and well-drained soil
Also good for: Foliage

Centaurea montana

The carpeting *C. montana* is the best-known perennial centaurea. It was the earliest to flower in our trial: mid-April in Leeds and Dorset. Their clumps of oval leaves spread rapidly to make effective ground cover. *C. montana* and its big, purple-flowered variety 'Parham' produced more leaf than the pale-pink *C. montana* 'Carnea' or white *C. montana* 'Alba', diluting the effect of the flowers. These all continued until late June or mid-July and were only mildly spoilt by rain opening up the centres of the plants. This variety may do better in a shadier spot as drought caused some wilting and crispy leaf tips in plants growing on the lighter soils at the height of summer. Nonetheless, *C. montana* put on an impressive second flush, often flowering until the frosts.

Height x spread: 45 x 60cm
Flowering period: May–June, July–August
chalky soil ☀
Also good for: Bees and butterflies

Geranium phaeum 'Lily Lovell'

'Lily Lovell' was in full bloom by mid-May at the majority of our test sites, making it the earliest of our geraniums to come into flower. *G. phaeum* is best known for tolerating deep shade, but 'Lily Lovell' also thrived in full sun in our trial. Its vigorous nature and large leaves (up to 20cm across) make it an excellent groundcover plant. But to control growth and prevent new seedlings overrunning your garden, it's best to cut back this geranium hard after flowering.

Height x spread: 120 x 110cm
Flowering period: May–June
chalky soil ☀ ◼
Also good for: Ground cover

Geranium sanguineum 'Blushing Turtle' ('Breathless')

The claims state that this geranium forms dense mounds of attractive green foliage and has great garden presence. Our three plants survived a harsh winter and produced vibrant pink flowers from May into summer. After a lull in August, flowering continued into December. Low growing and bushy with dark-green leaves, plants were easy to maintain and gave good ground cover.

Height x spread: 30 x 60cm
Flowering period: May–July, September–December

 chalky and well-drained soil
Also good for: Ground cover

> **Tip** Hardy geraniums may suffer from slugs and snail damage in spring. When new shoots appear, use organic slug pellets to stop them causing too much damage.

Geranium 'Mavis Simpson'

Usually we only recommend a variety if it does well at every test site. However, we thought 'Mavis Simpson' must get a mention. This low-growing plant with small, glossy, pink flowers and silver-green foliage was a strong favourite with our assessors. Unfortunately, it didn't like the cold and damp of our most northerly test site, where all three plants rotted off over winter. But if you live in a mild area, you can plant this geranium with confidence.

Height x spread: 40 x 140cm
Flowering period: June–August
chalky and well-drained soil
Also good for: Ground cover

Echinacea purpurea
'Coconut Lime' (see page 82)

Plants
for acid soil

An abundance of acid-loving plants, such as rhododendrons and camellias in neighbouring gardens, is usually a sure sign that the soil in your garden will be acid too. You can double check by using a soil test kit from the garden centre.

There is little that won't grow in soils that are only slightly acid, with a pH above 5.5, but if your pH is lower than that, it might be easier to only grow acid-tolerant plants.

You'll be able to enjoy many plants that gardeners in chalky areas can only dream of, such as azaleas, blue-flowered hydrangeas and summer-flowering heathers. Many fruits, such as blueberries and raspberries, also enjoy acid soils. Gardeners who don't have acid soils can only grow sickly specimens with yellowing leaves or have to grow them in containers filled with acidic ericaceous compost instead. Enjoy the soil you've got!

Pine needles and shredded Christmas trees make a useful mulch that will help to maintain the acidity. Many acidic soils are very sandy and so mulching is important as a way of helping to conserve moisture in these free-draining conditions.

If your soil is sandy, you will need to spread a fertiliser on the soil as these soils are often low in nutrients because they are washed out by the rain.

Heuchera 'Rachel'

'Rachel' flowered for a long time from June to October at our Leeds test site, its pink flowers much admired for the way they perfectly complemented its bronzed purple leaves. The quality of foliage was usually at its best in autumn after flowering, when colours intensified as the nights grew colder, and again in April or May once new leaves emerged. The foliage on 'Rachel' was excellent all year. Heucheras have a tendency to become woody with age, their leaves pushed higher out of the soil with an ugly bare stem beneath. Divide every three years into healthy shoots with a piece of stem that should root once replanted lower in the soil.

Height x spread: 45 x 50cm
Flowering period: June-October
acid soil ☀️ ▮
Also good for: Well-drained soil, Foliage, Bees and butterflies

Hosta 'Invincible'

With its glossy green leaves fanning out in a graceful circle, 'Invincible' was a very attractive plant that formed good-sized mounds at both trial gardens. Individual leaves were long and slender; their fresh olive-green colour enhanced by rippled edges. They flowered particularly well in London, and their flower stalks were just the right height for the size of the leaves. The flowers were white with a hint of lilac. Most of the plants had a few holes nibbled in them, but were generally fairly untroubled by slugs and snails in both trial gardens.

Height x spread: 25 x 25cm
Flowering period: July-August
acid soil ☀️ ▮
Also good for: Foliage, Scent

Geum 'Prinses Juliana'

In our north London trial, 'Prinses Juliana' was a particularly good early variety. Neither late ground frosts nor heavy rain showers damaged the blooms of our geums. This variety has a loose, open habit with flowering stems held high above the foliage. It excelled at all sites from May until early August, plus a second flush at Leeds and Dorset in autumn. The Leeds gardeners described it as being 'like 'Werner Arends' on steroids'! Give the plants a haircut in late winter to tidy them up. It will grow in most soils, except very dry ones.

Height x spread: 45 x 30cm
Flowering period: May–August
acid soil ☀ ▮
Also good for: Well-drained soil

Geranium x oxonianum 'A.T. Johnson'

There are wonderful silvery overtones to the light-pink flowers of 'A.T. Johnson', and they flower in abundance from early June through to August. This geranium retained its foliage over winter in milder areas, providing useful ground cover.
G. oxonianum and all its varieties should be cut back hard after the flowers become sparse to regenerate the foliage and give a second flush of flowers – but don't wait until the plant has gone completely to seed to do it.

Height x spread: 30 x 50cm
Flowering period: June–August
acid soil ☀
Also good for: Well-drained soil

Echinacea purpurea 'Coconut Lime'

This plant was a real winner in our trials, with a stunning display of lime-coloured, double flowers with orange cones that were lightly fringed with pure white petals. Plants flowered for weeks, even in long wet spells.

Height x spread: 70 x 60cm
Flowering period: July–September
`acid and well-drained soil` ☀
Also good for: Cottage garden borders

Echinacea paradoxa

E. paradoxa is the yellow-flowered parent of many of the new coneflower varieties. With its long stems and petals that hung like ribbons under the dark brown cones, this flower was elegant, if a little less showy than other varieties. Although the plant grows well in acid soil, it struggles in clay, unfortunately, as it prefers well-drained soil. A prairie plant, it is found growing wild in Missouri and Arkansas in the USA.

Height x spread: 65 x 50cm
Flowering period: July–August
`acid and well-drained soil` ☀
Also good for: Cottage garden borders

Tip Echinacea are magnets for bees and butterflies, and many also have a delicious scent. Their only drawback is that they tend to dislike heavy or wet soil and so might not survive over winter, but given a sunny spot and a moist but well-drained soil they can be easy to grow.

Crocosmia 'Emberglow'

Glowing buds of flame red, burnished orange or warm yellow erupt from slender leaves in late summer, with a vibrancy hard to replicate in any other plant. Some varieties have bronze and stiffly pleated foliage, providing additional architectural value from early summer until September. In our trials, 'Emberglow' challenged 'Lucifer' as the best red (see page 58). The crocosmias at our Glasgow site probably suffered most from winter wet. Smaller-flowered hybrids, such as 'Emberglow', that have *C. pottsii* (a stream dweller with red tubular flowers) in their blood are more tolerant of wet, and 'Emberglow' was among the survivors.

Height x spread: 70 x 10cm
Flowering period: August–September
`acid soil` :☀:
Also good for: Foliage

Rudbeckia fulgida var. *sullivantii* 'Goldsturm'

Three months in flower is a lot, but that's what you can expect from this gorgeous rudbeckia. It's a golden-flowered cracker, and once it comes into bloom it doesn't pause for breath until it finishes, which can often be as late as November. Unlike most rudbeckias, it's fully hardy, so you can look forward to the same show year after year. Best positioned near the front of the border. The classic partner for it is *Aster* x *frikartii* 'Mönch' (see page 73), which has lavender-coloured daisies that look beautiful against the yellow of the rudbeckia blooms.

Height x spread: 90 x 80cm
Flowering period: August–October
`acid soil` :☀:
Also good for: Clay soil, Well-drained soil, Cut flowers

Helleborus x *hybridus* 'Blue Lady' (see page 89)

Plants
for shade

Few plants will grow in total shade, but there is a good range to choose from where light reaches them for at least a short period in the day, which is best described as partial shade. Shade can then be subdivided into moist shade and damp shade.

Damp shade is actually shade without tree roots. It's not wet and it's not dry. Places you find damp shade include the north side of buildings or fences. In damp areas, even a few tree roots might share such conditions.

Many of the most luscious plants for damp shade come from areas with high rainfall and acid soils so you need to think about your soil pH and the requirements of the plant. Also, because a lot of the plants originate in damp woodland, many look their best in spring or early summer. So it's worth thinking about including some plants that look good in late summer and autumn too.

Dry shade, such as under trees, is much harder to find plants for, but there are some tough things that are up to the challenge, such as *Milium effusum* 'Aureum', *Cyclamen hederifolium* and, of course, ivy. Give them the best start that you can by digging in organic matter, such as garden compost, to improve the soil.

Hosta 'Dream Weaver'

This hosta was rated highly by all our trial assessors for its bold yellow variegation and quilted leaves. These leaves are heart-shaped and have dark blue-green margins that are broken up by a vivid splash of yellow in the middle – this faded to white later in the summer. The buds were variegated, too, opening to give a continuous display of white flowers from the beginning of June to mid-July, then sporadically into September in the London garden. Slug or snail damage was visible on most plants from May and, though not bad on the whole, became quite severe on one plant in the group that had the early drench of liquid slug control in north London. You could plant this hosta with a hellebore, such as Corsican hellebore, *Helleborus argutifolius*, which will flower much earlier but have equally bold leaves, and make full use of its potential width by planting it as ground cover in a shady area.

Height x spread: 30 x 60cm
Flowering period: June–July
`moist soil` 🔆 ▮
Also good for: Foliage

Monarda 'Squaw'

This plant looks great – its bright trumpet flowers sprout from a hub at the top of each stem, and appear over a long period. In fact, when the flowers have finished the spent hubs still look attractive, even if the bees have lost interest in them by then. 'Squaw' is less susceptible to mildew than some other monarda varieties.

Height x spread: 110 x 60cm
Flowering period: July–September
`well-drained soil` 🔆 ▮
Also good for: Bees and butterflies

Veronicastrum virginicum

Veronicastrum virginicum has a wonderful architectural presence with stalks up to 2m tall topped by mauve flower spires. The leaves are held in cartwheels, almost at right angles to the strictly vertical stems. Despite its height, it stands up well to winds and rarely needs staking. It is a useful late-summer plant, and likes moist, fertile soil in the sun or partial shade. The white variety 'Album' has stems tinged with bronze, while the shorter 'Pink Glow' grows to just 1m. They are reliably hardy – a spot in full sun or dappled shade will keep them happy. The species are easy to grow from seed, though *Veronicastrum* does benefit from a cold period, so sow in late winter in an unheated greenhouse.

Height x spread: 2m x 50cm
Flowering period: August–September
moist soil
Also good for: Late summer flowers

Hacquetia epipactis

This charming little woodland plant isn't so obviously a member of the umbellifer family. Its clusters of flowers are tiny in comparison to most umbels, and backed by green bracts that look like petals. The flowers are luminous yellow and they covered the pin-cushion plants from late February in our trials. Fresh green foliage started to grow as the flowers faded, but in the colder Scottish winter they struggled a bit, seeming happier in the milder locations. Surround them with daffodils under a tree for a bright start to spring.

Height x spread: 20 x 30cm
Flowering period: February–May
moist soil
Also good for: Winter flowers

Papaver orientale 'Patty's Plum'

This must be one of the most well-known oriental poppies and caused quite a sensation when it was introduced at the Chelsea Flower Show in the late 1990s. The lush bronzed purple of the pleated petals brings antique silk to mind, although the colour faded in strong sunshine – plant it in dappled shade to preserve its extraordinary colour for longer. Also, all of our plants had to be supported. It didn't re-flower in either trial garden but after giving us more than a month of stunning colour, it was rated highly by all of our assessors. It would look lovely surrounded by the white flowers of *Camassia leichtlinii* 'Alba' (also called *C.* subsp. *suksdorfii* 'Alba'), which does well in some shade. Cut back the whole plant when the flowers have faded.

Height x spread: 90 x 60cm
Flowering period: May–June
clay and well-drained soil
Also good for: Cottage garden borders

Helleborus x *hybridus* 'Blue Lady'

The abundant, dark, nodding flowers of 'Blue Lady' caught everyone's eye in our trials. They weren't actually blue but purple (flower colour and shape vary slightly as these plants are grown from seed), and were produced on a cluster of bare, upright stems in late winter. The flowers were followed by dark green leaves, which can be cut to the ground again in early winter before the next set of flowering stems emerge.

Height x spread: 35 x 30cm
Flowering period: January–May
well-drained soil ☀ ■
Also good for: Clay soil

Helleborus x *nigercors*

Even though *H.* x *nigercors* is only subtly coloured, the large, outward-looking flowers really caught the eye in our trial. It flowered over a long period at all our test sites and had evergreen leaves, which would give a good period of interest in the border. Remove some of the low, sprawling leaves in autumn, including the ones nearest to the ground, as thinning will help keep plants healthy.

Height x spread: 30 x 60cm
Flowering period: January–April
well-drained soil ☀ ■
Also good for: Bees and butterflies

> **Tip** To admire the flowers of *Helleborus* x *hybridus* at their best and avoid hellebore leaf spot disease, cut off all the leaves in December and mulch around the plant.

Carex morrowii 'Fisher's Form'

One of the earliest sedges to flower, this sturdy little evergreen started to produce spikes of tufty, white, female flowers topped by black male flowers from February on one test site, and between March and April on the others – again, the timing depends on the weather. The leaves were sword-shaped and fresh green with creamy yellow edges. They were popular with all our assessors. It looked handsome all year round and is one of the easiest to grow, especially if you have a moist shady spot, perhaps alongside ferns or hostas. 'Fisher's Form' also grows happily in a container for a shady spot.

Height x spread: 35 x 55cm
Flowering period: February–April
moist soil
Also good for: Foliage, Containers

Milium effusum 'Aureum'

This plant produced billowing sprays of pinky-brown flowers and leaves that can look coarse but improve after flowering. 'Aureum' is primarily grown for its golden leaves, which are invaluable for brightening up a shady spot. It will grow in most soils and is especially useful in dry shade.

Height x spread: 90 x 70cm
Flowering period: June
moist and well-drained soil
Also good for: Foliage

Luzula sylvatica 'Marginata'
This plant produced billowing sprays of
pinky-brown flowers and leaves that can
look coarse but improve after flowering.

Height x spread: 60 x 60cm
Flowering period: May–June
`moist soil`
Also good for: Foliage

Gladiolus 'Gwendolyn' (see page 98)

Plants
for sun

Sun is essential for plants to make food by converting its energy using photosynthesis, so it's not surprising that so many plants thrive in a sunny spot. Tender and half-hardy plants often prefer a sunny site and you may be surprised by how hardy something 'exotic' proves to be in your garden.

South-facing positions get sun all day, while east-facing ones are sunny in the morning and shady in the afternoon, and west-facing ones are the opposite.

A quick word of warning for east-facing spots is to avoid planting anything that's on the tender side there as the harsh sunlight melting any frost in the morning can cause damage. Camellia flowers are particularly vulnerable to this, often turning brown when planted in an east-facing spot. The glare of the sun dries out the soil more quickly than in shady areas, so take care to cover the soil surface in spring with a layer of mulch to help conserve the moisture. Clay soils often crack in a dry, sunny spot and sandy soils can become bone dry.

Make sure you soak the rootball of plants in a bucket of water before planting and water them during dry weather for the first few months to help them establish.

Full sun plus crowded conditions can result in plants that collapse just as they reach flowering size or when a gusty wind blows, so make sure you plant at the recommended spacing for your plants.

Dahlia 'Weston Pirate'

The top choice in our trials: plants were extremely bushy and covered with masses of small cactus-type flowers. A small stake was enough to keep them heading in the right direction and a quick deadheading each week kept them blooming well. Their sumptuous flowers worked really well in mixed flower arrangements and lasted for at least five days. Dahlias are tender perennials so must be protected from frost. On light soils, simply leave the tubers in the ground and cover them with a 10–15cm layer of mulch in autumn. On heavier soils, it's best to lift them and store in a frost-free place.

Height x spread: 100 x 60cm
Flowering period: July–October
moist soil ☀
Also good for: Cut flowers

Dahlia 'Pam Howden'

This is a beautiful dahlia, and from the moment the plants in our test started to flower they drew plenty of admirers. They were easy to grow and, being quite short, didn't need staking. They gave us lots of large water-lily-type flowers with a gorgeous metallic hue. The cut flowers looked good for seven days and would look brilliant floating singly in a bowl. To get larger flowers with longer stems, remove the side-shoots from either side of the large central bud and repeat down the stem.

Height x spread: 70 x 65cm
Flowering period: July–October
`moist soil` ☀
Also good for: Cut flowers

Papaver orientale 'Curlilocks'

You certainly won't miss the flowers of 'Curlilocks'. If their vibrant colouring doesn't attract your attention, the size of their shaggy flowers will. The double layer of petals, with edges that looked like they'd been cut into strips, held their shape well in the wind and rain of late May in both our test gardens, and none of our plants needed to be staked. Black blotches, 'eyelash' markings on petal backs and black stamens in the centre added to the charms of this very eye-catching plant. It was very similar to 'Turkenlouis', also in the trial, but flowered for about a week longer. You'd need to team this with other vibrant plants such as the foxtail lily (*Eremurus* x *isabellinus* Ruiter Hybrids), or use it as an accent plant among evergreen shrubs.

Height x spread: 80 x 60cm
Flowering period: May–early June
`clay and well-drained soil` ☀
Also good for: Late spring flowers

Sun

Diascia 'Little Tango'

Diascias prefer a position in full sun and warm conditions for the best flowering. They can be used in pots or baskets, but would be just as happy cascading down a rockery. Diascias aren't fully hardy so are often grown as annuals, but they can survive mild winters if you protect them. 'Little Tango' flowered strongly all summer during our trials, providing us with a haze of vibrant flowers. The plants were shorter and tended to spread horizontally. As autumn approached they began to wane, producing fewer flowers and a diminished display.

Height x spread: 25 x 40cm, trailing 10cm
Flowering period: June–September
`well-drained soil` :☀:
Also good for: Containers

Diascia 'Breezee Apple Blossom'

Similar to the others we tried from the Breezee Series, this was a small and later flowering variety. Plants were quite short and stout and didn't trail much. However, they did give us an excellent display, with large flowers that lasted really well. As they come from drier climes, diascias don't need massive amounts of water; they don't like to have their feet wet and will benefit from good drainage.

Height x spread: 20 x 35cm, trailing 5cm
Flowering period: June–September
`well-drained soil` :☀:
Also good for: Containers

Tip If diascias are set back by poor weather or flowering slows, trim them with a pair of shears and add a liquid feed. They should flower again in a couple of weeks.

Campanula poscharskyana 'E.H. Frost'

Evergreen plants are always useful, and although the heart-shaped leaves were straggly after the snow melted in our Glasgow site, in our north London site the small mounds looked neat all year round. In spring, the new growth was a lovely light green and then masses of star-shaped, almost white flowers appeared and kept appearing for months. Our plants kept their mounded shape and didn't spread far. 'E.H. Frost' would look pretty next to a path. If it begins to spread too far or looks untidy, simply dig out any bits you don't want or cut it back hard.

Height x spread: 60 x 35cm
Flowering period: June–September
moist or well-drained soil ☼ ▮
Also good for: Ground cover

Cosmos bipinnatus 'Candy Stripe'

The picotee edges of the petals really enhanced the pretty flowers of this variety. The candy shades of the small flowers, held on upright stems, varied in our tests from white with pink markings to pale pink with darker pink edges and centres, but they weren't stripy as their name suggested. The number of flowers on each plant meant that lots of deadheading was needed. This variety would work well with similar-coloured oriental poppies (*Papaver orientale*); the cosmos leaves and blooms would take over as poppies faded.

Height x spread: 130 x 80cm
Flowering period: June–August
well-drained soil ☼
Also good for: Bees and butterflies

Gladiolus 'Sancerre'

Large, crisp white flowers with creamy throats packed the tall spikes of 'Sancerre', to give us one of the most stunning and long-lasting displays of our whole trial. There were plenty of side spikes with extra flowers, and they remained reasonably tidy as flower-opening travelled towards the tip. Their height meant they tended to lean and we staked quite a few. When it comes to staking, bamboo canes and string will do the job. Tie the stems at intervals along their length, so that they don't bend from the tied point. Feed with a tomato food once flower spikes appear.

Height x spread: 150 x 25cm
Flowering period: August–October
well-drained soil ☀
Also good for: Foliage, Cut flowers

Gladiolus 'Gwendolyn'

Our assessors loved the restrained style of this variety. The flowers are medium-sized and a stunning bright-plum colour, set off by white margins that make them look permanently backlit. The elegant purplish stems complement the flower colour and didn't need staking, and the finished flowers shrivelled up without detracting from the rest of the display. Water well during dry spells and weed regularly.

Height x spread: 110 x 25cm
Flowering period: August–September
well-drained soil ☀
Also good for: Foliage, Cut flowers

> **Tip** Photographs always show gladioli obediently facing front, but we found the flowers develop in random directions – they might present their best face to your fence!

Crocosmia x crocosmiiflora 'Emily McKenzie'

Crocosmias have glowing buds of flame red, burnished orange or warm yellow erupting from slender leaves in late summer, with a vibrancy hard to replicate in any other plant. 'Emily McKenzie' has open stars of golden yellow that fold back on themselves in warm weather. By the middle of August and early September, this large-flowered variety is at its best. The blooms persisted well into September at all sites, and were still going strong in October at our Beverley and north London sites. Divide plants between November and June.

Height x spread: 60 x 10cm
Flowering period: August–September
moist or well-drained soil ☀
Also good for: Foliage

Crocosmia x crocosmiiflora 'Solfatare'

'Solfatare' is a bronze-leaved form with stiffly pleated foliage, providing good architectural value. These jewels of southern Africa shoot from underground corms, but are best bought as actively growing perennials. By autumn, most foliage in our tests had died down with the first heavy frost. One way to limit the damage to less-hardy varieties is to plant them more deeply, about 5cm lower than the soil level in the pot. All our test sites followed this advice and it did seem to work, because none of the four in England lost more than one or two plants in the whole trial. Feed with a handful of Growmore in spring.

Height x spread: 60 x 10cm
Flowering period: August–September
moist or well-drained soil ☀
Also good for: Foliage

Allium 'Pinball Wizard'

This had some of the largest flowers on our trial – a whopping 15cm across. Thankfully they were held on thick, strong stems that were able to carry their weight. Flower heads were mid-purple and as they weren't densely packed with star-shaped flowers they had the appearance of fluffy, purple mohair! Not as many bulbs came up as we'd hoped, but those that did were attention-grabbers and looked fabulous in April–June. Plant bulbs in autumn about 20cm apart and at two-and-a-half times their own depth. Alliums aren't too fussy, but a sheltered spot with in full sun is ideal.

Height x spread: 95 x 100cm
Flowering period: April–June
`well-drained soil` ☀
Also good for: Seed heads

Allium karataviense

This allium still has spherical flower heads, but plants reach just 25cm high and have broad, strap-like leaves that remain grey-green until the flowers are over. Generally allium leaves become untidy in early summer, but not so with *A. karataviense* at some of our trials, the leaves of which remained green, apart from some mottling from rust in June. The good-sized blooms were whitish-pink with dusky-pink centres and were held on short, purple stems. Plant these diminutive alliums close together at the front of a border or in a pot. Alliums are hardy in the UK and can be left in the ground year round.

Height x spread: 25 x 30cm
Flowering period: May–July
`well-drained soil` ☀
Also good for: Seed heads

Allium 'Ambassador'

This superb variety had a long season of interest in our tests. Flowers appeared each year between May and June and continued until July, and were followed by very attractive, architectural seedheads that persisted throughout August until the flowering stems became detached at their bases. The dense, mid-purple flower heads rose above the trial bed on very tall, strong stems. These weren't particularly uniform, but they remained upright throughout summer. With its lovely seedheads this is a particularly useful allium for cut flower displays; remove finished flowers and leave a natural colour or spray the dry heads silver or gold. To keep alliums tidy, gather up the dead leaves in early summer.

Height x spread: 150 x 25cm
Flowering period: August–October
`well-drained soil` ☼
Also good for: Bees and butterflies

Festuca glauca 'Elijah Blue'

In our trial, we found that the main attraction of these little bun-shaped fescues were the endearing spiky mounds of blue leaves that lasted all year round. Sunny borders would suit them best. The spiky blue foliage looks good all year but particularly towards the end of the year when it was enhanced first by dew and then by winter frosts. It's a stunning plant for a gravel garden, the front of a formal border or in a container. If plants are beginning to look untidy, cut back the old leaves by about a third while the plant is actively growing, from April to July.

Height x spread: 55 x 50cm
`well-drained soil` ☼
Also good for: Foliage

Agapanthus 'Northern Star'

This is a classic agapanthus, with clumps of short strappy leaves and cobalt-blue flowers with a prominent darker stripe in the middle. In our trials, the tall stems tended to be a bit floppy, but they were great favourites at both sites all the same.

Height x spread: 90 x 70cm
Flowering period: July–August
`well-drained soil` ☀
Also good for: Gravel gardens

Alstroemeria 'Little Miss Rosalind'

All the 'Little Miss' varieties produced very short and compact mounds of colour in our trials, though we found that our 'Little Miss Rosalind' plants varied a bit, in that some spread themselves out. Agapanthus are often recommended as good pot plants: ours not only survived the winter in a pot in north London, but flourished, trailing prettily over the sides the following year. The bright-pink flowers were as large as those on taller plants, though they produced slightly fewer of them in Glasgow than in north London.

Height x spread: 25 x 40cm
Flowering period: June–September
`well-drained soil` ☀
Also good for: Containers

Scabiosa atropurpurea 'Ace of Spades'

In our trial, black buds opened into velvety purple-red flowers that were darker than 'Black Cat'. Blue-green at the start of summer, the leaves gradually turned bright green, complementing the blooms. Scabious is often called the pincushion flower and it's easy to see why; the flower heads are made up of many tiny blooms that look as though they have pins sticking out of them. This variety bloomed for 12 weeks in our trial.

Height x spread: 80 x 55cm
Flowering period: June–August
`well-drained soil` ☀
Also good for: Bees and butterflies

Scabiosa caucasica 'Fama'

With huge (10cm) flowers varying from deep indigo to pale blue-violet, 'Fama' was a favourite perennial among our testers. The plants stood straighter than most in our trial. It would make a lovely addition to a vase of cut flowers. It bloomed for 10 weeks in our trial.

Height x spread: 95 x 45cm
Flowering period: June–August
`well-drained soil` ☀
Also good for: Bees and butterflies

> **Tip** Scabious do not always germinate easily, so sow plenty of seed to get enough plants. Sow 3mm deep in seed compost, preferably in a heated propagator at 20°C. Prick out seedlings into individual pots or modules and grow on in the greenhouse. Plant out after all risk of frost has passed in late spring.

Zinnia 'Zahara Yellow'

This is a modern hybrid, so seed was a bit more expensive, but it was a cut above most of the other plants we trialled. The neat domes of foliage were covered in a myriad of small flowers, which lasted really well and only needed a little deadheading. They also successfully fended off powdery mildew much better than many other varieties. A flawless plant, and without doubt our top choice. The Zahara Series is available in many colours that should perform similarly. It flowered for 16 weeks in our trial. Keep plants deadheaded to ensure a constant supply of flowers.

Height x spread: 30 x 40cm
Flowering period: June–September
`well-drained soil` ☀
Also good for: Cut flowers

Zinnia 'Starlight Rose'

A modern hybrid, our plants were uniform in size, compact and seemed to flower forever. They quickly filled their space with an array of bright, bicoloured flowers. Plants were unaffected by powdery mildew and the strong winds that damaged many of the other varieties we were trialling. It's no wonder this plant is already an All American Selection award winner. Zinnias are easy to grow from seed and can be sown directly into the soil in May. However, they can germinate poorly, so start them in modules in the greenhouse. Sow two seeds per cell. They should germinate in 3–7 days. Pull out the weaker of the two seedlings per cell and plant in a sunny position in May.

Height x spread: 35 x 50cm
Flowering period: June–September
`well-drained soil` ☀
Also good for: Cut flowers

Zinnia Lilliput mix

'Lilliput' has been around as a seed mix for almost a century now, and has evidently stood the test of time well. It was easy to grow in our tests and gave an excellent display for longer than many of the other varieties on test. The plants eventually became quite large, and were covered with a copious number of small single and double flowers in a wide mix of colours. They put on a great show, looking fantastic for 14 weeks before they eventually began to succumb to powdery mildew in October. If plants do become infected, you can spray them with a garden fungicide to reduce the spread of disease.

Height x spread: 60 x 50cm
Flowering period: June–August
well-drained soil ☀
Also good for: Cut flowers

Zinnia 'Giant Wine Bouquet' (see page 111)

Exotic-looking
plants

Many of us long to grow plants with the dramatic shapes and bright colours that remind us of holidays abroad. While it's true that many exotic-looking plants are tender and need protection from the frost, there are also a surprising number that match the bill, which are perfectly hardy in the UK.

If you're tempted by the tender kinds, a number of them can be grown from seed, cuttings and divisions. Many can be raised in the greenhouse then hardened off in a cold frame, gradually acclimatising them to lower temperatures over two weeks before planting outside in June. For best results, most exotics will need a well-drained and sunny bed. Some can be left in the ground over winter, protected by a dry mulch in autumn or by wrapping with fleece. Others need to be lifted before the frosts damage them and brought indoors to spend the winter in a frost-free place.

Whichever plants you choose to grow, combine brightly-coloured flowers with large and strikingly-shaped leaves, such as fatsias, phormiums and cordylines for a jungle look. While it may involve a bit of effort to give your garden an exotic feel, it's great fun as you can change the look of your planting scheme each year and it will never be accused of being dull!

Tulipa 'Irene Parrot'

'Irene Parrot' was bred from the very popular and reliable tulip 'Prinses Irene'. It has mid-sized flowers that are frilled, cut and flamed to give it a really exotic look. Unlike other parrot-type tulips, it didn't flop under the weight of heavy rain during our trial and continued to flower for 31 days. It would look best with yellow, orange or red tulips in a zesty display. Plant tulips deeply (about 30cm deep) and they should be more likely to flower for several years.

Height: 25cm
Flowering period: April
well-drained soil
Also good for: Cut flowers

Dahlia 'Lorona Dawn'

Unlike any other dahlias we tested, this has novel 'windmill' type flowers. They proved a hit with visitors, who thought they were unusually attractive, and were great as cut flowers, lasting for at least six days. They weren't too thuggish and would look great in herbaceous borders. Our plants began to suffer with mildew in late September. Dahlias are often grown from tubers, but growing them from cuttings will give excellent results, with little difference in the size of plants by the end of the year.

Height x spread: 105 x 60cm
Flowering period: August–October
`rich moist soil` ☀
Also good for: Cut flowers

Dahlia 'Jamaica'

A real dazzler. The short, compact plants had no need for staking in our trial and were covered from late July onwards with masses of small, decorative flowers. Their strongly contrasting flowers quickly turned brown at the edges as they aged, so they needed regular deadheading to stay looking tidy. Cut flowers lasted for at least four days. Watch out for slugs while plants are small and earwigs, which shred the petals of new flowers.

Height x spread: 75 x 60cm
Flowering period: July–September
`rich moist soil` ☀
Also good for: Cut flowers

Tip To get larger flowers with longer stems, remove the side-shoots from either side of the large central bud. Repeat down the stem to ensure all of the plant's energy is focused on producing a few large blooms.

Exotic-looking plants

Kniphofia northiae

The rosettes of broad, pointed leaves of *K. northiae* are very different from any other variety we trialled. They flower much earlier than other varieties, too, producing fat flower heads of bright red-orange over creamy yellow buds. Kniphofias like a sunny spot and deep soil that stays moist in summer but is on the dry side during winter. Mulch with a 5–8cm layer of well-rotted, organic matter in late autumn to help provide some protection during winter.

Height x spread: 110 x 100cm
Flowering period: April–May
`well-drained soil` ☀
Also good for: Bees and butterflies

Cosmos sulphureus 'Polidor Mixed'

Our tests showed that although 'Polidor Mixed' was very tall (around 120cm), it didn't lean over and didn't need staking. This giant produced semi-double flowers on long stems that pointed in many different directions. The dark green leaves gave a great contrast to the fiery orange blooms. The mixture should contain flowers of yellow and different shades of orange but once we had sown, pricked out and planted our 'Polidor Mixed', we were left with only orange-flowered plants. However, bees of many kinds were attracted to them. Another bonus was that deadheading, although it would prolong flowering, wasn't necessary to keep the plants looking good. Take advantage of their height and use them at the back of a border.

Height x spread: 120 x 120cm
Flowering period: July–September
`well-drained soil` ☀ ▮
Also good for: Bees and butterflies

Zinnia 'Giant Wine Bouquet'

This was a bit different from most of the other zinnias we grew in our trial and produced large plants with gorgeously deep-coloured, fully double flowers on very long and thick stems. Unfortunately, some plants suffered with leaf spots and a few were damaged by high winds, but they recovered well to put on a fantastic display. Despite being slightly sensitive, they were extremely beautiful. Make sure they have enough space to grow: closely planted groups will be more susceptible to powdery mildew. If plants do become infected, you can spray them with a garden fungicide.

Height x spread: 75 x 50cm
Flowering period: July–September
`well-drained soil` :☀:
Also good for: Cut flowers

Passiflora 'Perfume Passion'

This plant claims to have abundant, exotic flowers with the fragrance of jasmine and orange fruits in late summer. We found that it doesn't require very much maintenance, but is tender. The multicoloured, complex blooms of 'Perfume Passion' would have impressed us even without the added bonus of scent. The perfume was a mixture of ginger and lily, rather than jasmine. With three-pointed leaves and attractive curly tendrils, our plants ranged over their supports. There were rarely several flowers out at once, but there was a steady stream of stunning blooms. We didn't get any fruit, though. We placed ours in a large pot and brought it inside before autumn frosts.

Height x spread: 160 x 160cm
Flowering period: June–October
`well-drained and dry soil` :☀:
Also good for: Scent

Amaranthus tricolour 'Illumination'

Amaranthus grows in many tropical regions around the world. This variety has colourful leaves rather than flowers and resembles a poinsettia. Our plants progressed through an ever-changing display of purple with splashes of red, yellow, orange and an extraordinarily vivid raspberry-pink over the course of the summer. The display was every bit as vibrant as we'd hoped, and was easy to grow from seed, germinating readily and growing quickly into sturdy plants. Plant with *Pennisetum glaucum* 'Jester' and *Rudbeckia* 'Cherokee Sunset'.

Height x spread: 100 x 50cm
Flowering period: July–September
`well-drained soil` ☀
Also good for: Containers

Eccremocarpus scaber

Quick growing and very bright, this climbing plant germinated easily and, once out in the bed, it quickly scrambled to the top of the arch on which we grew it. It produced its long stems of light-orange trumpet flowers with yellow tips for weeks, and was vigorous without ever getting out of control. The dark-green leaves were also pretty, and the tendrils, curling out from all over the plants, added to its slightly wild appeal. As its common name, Chilean glory vine, suggests, eccremocarpus originates in South America, but it's often hardy in Britain, especially in the south. Plant *Eccremocarpus scaber* with *Asclepias curassavica* and *Ricinus communis* 'Gibsonii'.

Height x spread: 200 x 50cm
Flowering period: June–October
`well-drained soil` ☀
Also good for: Containers

Alstroemeria 'Inca Ice'

The slightly faded look to the pink in these flowers, along with the glaucous colour of the leaves, gave 'Inca Ice' a more subdued glamour than some of the brighter varieties. Pretty pink buds and petal-backs added a rosy glow. Our plants were vigorous and bushy, producing a mass of sturdy stems that never needed support.

A favourite with all our assessors, they also coped well with the extremes of drought and heavy rain, and were one of the least affected by late-spring frosts.

Height x spread: 80 x 110cm
Flowering period: June–October
`well-drained soil` ☀
Also good for: Cut flowers

Sedum telephium 'Gooseberry Fool' (see page 118)

Plants
for bees and butterflies

Many plants are a magnet for wildlife, in particular birds, bees, butterflies and other insects. Butterflies are perhaps the most popular thanks to their colourful wings, but bees are incredibly useful as they act as a pollinator for many plants, ensuring that we can enjoy great crops of many fruit and vegetables.

Despite a general decline, six species of bumblebee are still common almost everywhere, including gardens. It's thought that gardens are attractive to bees because they have lots of boundaries, such as hedges, fences and garden buildings, which are suitable for nesting, as well as compost heaps, bird boxes and flowerbeds. There's also often plenty of nectar and pollen from flowers well into autumn.

Bumblebees are still in decline, however, and three species have become extinct. Bumblebees need two things: nesting sites and flowers. Most gardeners are pretty good at providing the flowers from March to September.

Choose single- rather than double-flowered varieties, as the latter produce little or no pollen and nectar. Also plant a selection of species with overlapping blooming periods, so the food supply is continuous. Bees like nesting in undisturbed areas, so if you can leave a corner of lawn rough and undisturbed – behind a garage or shed, for example – that is ideal.

Zinnia 'Old Mexico'

With its spreading growth and narrow, hairy leaves, 'Old Mexico' is likely to have a similar heritage to 'Aztec Sunset' (see page 64). In our trial, they developed into low, mounded plants with lots of small single flowers on short stems, in a mix of flame-coloured blends. We also noted that they were much loved by bees, which hummed all around them. Our plants remained unscathed by high winds and managed to stay mildew-free until autumn, despite a cool, wet summer.

Height x spread: 45 x 55cm
Flowering period: July–September
well-drained soil ☀
Also good for: Cut flowers

Dahlia 'Magenta Star'

The dark foliage on this black-leafed dahlia contrasts wonderfully with its bright pink flowers. Our plants needed only minimal support, so it would be well suited to herbaceous borders, and the single flowers hummed with insects. In the end, it was the plants' striking contrasts that secured them as firm favourites with visitors to our trial site. Dahlias are hungry plants so like a rich soil in a sunny, sheltered spot. Dig in garden compost before planting.

Height x spread: 100 x 60cm
Flowering period: July–October
`moist soil` ☀
Also good for: Cut flowers

Dahlia 'Keith's Pet'

These diminutive plants were the first to start flowering and continued to do so for 12 weeks. The small single flowers looked great against the dark, feathery foliage. Our plants didn't need support and were a big hit with wildlife. Flowering stopped in late September when powdery mildew caught hold. Cuttings are usually available by mail order during April. When they arrive, pot them into large containers that hold at least 1 litre (don't use cold compost as it can give them a shock, causing a check in growth), then grow in a frost-free location until they're ready to plant out in late May.

Height x spread: 65 x 55cm
Flowering period: July–September
`moist soil` ☀
Also good for: Cut flowers

Bees and butterflies

Sedum 'Autumn Joy'

Also known as 'Herbstfreude', this is a classic sedum with big, jagged-edged leaves and strong stems topped with large heads of pink and red flowers. In our trial, the plant that was given the Chelsea chop became a neat ball of buds, which erupted into colour. The 'Chelsea Chop' involves cutting plants back by about a third to a half of their height in May. This promotes bushier growth and can stop some perennial plants from flopping, though it also tends to lead to smaller leaves and flowers.

Height x spread: 55 x 90cm
Flowering period: August–October
`well-drained soil` ☀
Also good for: Foliage

Sedum telephium 'Gooseberry Fool'

With a loose shape and varied stem heights, this reminded one assessor of a group of mini Scots pine trees! The green-white flowers are an unusual twist on the classic sedum. It's worth doing the Chelsea chop on this one (see above): our chopped plant not only had a better shape, it was covered in fizzy green flowers, too. Plant in well-drained soil in a sunny position. The sun not only improves flowering and shape, but often leaf colour, especially in darker leaves like this variety.

Height x spread: 75 x 110cm
Flowering period: August–October
`well-drained soil` ☀
Also good for: Winter effect

Lavandula angustifolia 'Melissa Lilac'

A recently introduced variety with dense, chubby spikes of pale blue flowers, which lit up the mound of grey-green felty leaves for weeks in our trial. Our plants were compact and the flower spikes strong and upright. Lavender does best in well-drained soils with plenty of sunshine. Wet soil in winter is as likely to kill plants as the cold. In the first year, remove spent flower heads and the top 2.5cm of growth once flowering is finished. In subsequent years, cut plants back to 25cm from the base (as long as there is leafy growth below this level) to keep them from becoming woody. Complete pruning before the end of August.

Height x spread: 50 x 60cm
Flowering period: June–August
well-drained soil ☀
Also good for: Foliage, Scent

Lavandula angustifolia 'Folgate'

Not as well known as it deserves to be, our assessors agreed that the long and widely spaced flowers on upright spikes had a hazy purple colour, but still had fantastic impact, set off by green leaves. If you spot a shiny, metallic-looking, purple-and-green-striped beetle on your lavender, don't stop to admire it. Adult beetles may be spotted in the spring and early summer, but once their eggs hatch into slug-like larvae in late summer, adults and grubs attack the shoot tips and flowers. Plants may recover, but it's best to remove beetles by hand as soon as they're spotted, or use a spray.

Height x spread: 55 x 60cm
Flowering period: June–July
well-drained soil ☀
Also good for: Foliage, Scent

Cosmos bipinnatus 'Psyche White'

This variety produced some of the biggest flowers in our trial. They varied from singles to semi-doubles. We noticed that the bees visiting this variety were honeybees rather than bumblebees. Some plants on the edge of the plot leaned a little, but you could prevent this by supporting with pea sticks. Deadhead for fresh blooms and watch for powdery mildew in September. It is easily raised from seed.

Height x spread: 110 x 100cm
Flowering period: July
`well-drained soil` ☀ ▮
Also good for: Cut flowers

Scabiosa atropurpurea 'Oxford Blue'

'Oxford Blue' really stood out from the other varieties in our trial due to the big (7.5cm) flowers that started off flat and gradually changed into a tall dome. They were teaming with bees and hoverflies throughout the summer. For a big display, it's cheaper to raise plants from seed. Sow indoors in spring and move the seedlings to individual pots. Plant them out once the danger of frost has passed in late spring.

Height x spread: 80 x 85cm
Flowering period: June–August
`well-drained soil` ☀
Also good for: Cut flowers

Tip Most scabious plants are blousy rather than tidy, so they fit into cottage-garden plantings better than formal areas. The flowers can be complemented by planting them with other plants of a similar shade.

Allium sphaerocephalon

When most of the other alliums in our trial were going over, *A. sphaerocephalon* was just coming into its own, so it's brilliant for later summer colour. The bright, pinkish-purple, drumstick-shaped flowers were held in abundance on stems that were strong but flexible. This gave a very natural and graceful appearance. Flowering was fairly consistent at both of our trial sites, continuing from June to August. As is common among alliums, this variety was extremely popular with bees and hoverflies.

Height x spread: 90 x 30cm
Flowering period: June–August
well-drained soil ☀
Also good for: Gravel gardens

Potentilla recta 'Warrenii'

If you want a plant that will just go on and on producing flowers, this one is for you. From year one, 'Warrenii' stood out as the longest flowering of the potentillas on trial, going on for an average of 14 weeks in its first year and 22 weeks in its second (that's five weeks more than the next best here). The flowers were a bright, buttery yellow and stood out well against the green foliage. It's a beautiful, simple plant and would suit a naturalistic planting scheme. Grow alongside other supporting plants – red or yellow potentillas go well with dahlias, heleniums, ornamental grasses and dark-leafed cannas. Pink potentillas would look lovely with purple sage, meadowsweet (filipendula), agastache and sedum.

Height x spread: 55 x 60cm
Flowering period: July–October
 well-drained soil ☀

Also good for: Cottage garden borders

Nepeta racemosa 'Walker's Low'

Although this is a variety of catmint it's not the sort that cats like to lounge on – the furry visitors it's more likely to attract are bees. It has aromatic grey-green foliage and long spikes of small blue flowers. It actually comes into bloom in early summer but it flowers so freely that it's just as good in late summer. You'll need to stake it when you plant it. Bees seem to love it and the flowers are alive with activity during summer.

Height x spread: 50 x 60cm
Flowering period: June–October
well-drained soil ☼
Also good for: Foliage, Scent

Penstemon 'Schoenholzeri'

This variety is sometimes also labelled as 'Firebird' and is well worth looking out for. Its vibrant trumpet flowers are freely produced, and will give you a long show of colour. It's great in the border but is just as good in containers. It's one of the toughest penstemons there is, and will survive the winter in most gardens. Bees seem to love the flowers. Overall penstemon are unfussy plants as long as the soil is well drained. They'll grow in full sun and partial shade.

Height x spread: 90 x 90cm
Flowering period: July–October
well-drained soil ☼◼
Also good for: Containers

Tip Butterflies prefer a sheltered spot as they don't like being buffeted by the wind so try to include fencing or hedging in your garden. They also need a sunny spot and somewhere they can access water to drink.

Erigeron glaucus 'Sea Breeze' (see page 129)

Plants
for coastal gardens

Many of us dream of living by the sea, but gardening by the sea presents a challenge as plants must be able to stand up to the salty air, winds blowing in from the sea, which blacken leaves, and often free-draining soil.

Wind is perhaps the biggest enemy of coastal gardeners as it comes roaring in straight off the sea. Getting a windbreak in place is essential. Wind netting and fencing provide a quick solution, but for longer-term planting, tough shrubs, such as tamarisk, olearia and privet, as a shelter belt not only works well but looks good too.

A windbreak needs to filter the wind and reduce its speed, rather than blocking it. Solid barriers such as walls can often do more damage as the wind comes down with full force on the other side of them. Salt combined with wind burns and blackens leaves. Some plants are better at coping with this assault than others.

Western coastal gardens are kept virtually frost free thanks to the Gulf stream, so with a decent wind break many tender plants can be grown successfully thanks to the mild temperatures.

Seaside soils can also be a challenge as they tend to be free-draining and quick to dry out. Choosing plants that are better suited to good drainage and also mulching them regularly with organic matter, such as garden compost, to conserve moisture will all help.

Achillea 'Coronation Gold'

Achilleas make a bold statement in herbaceous borders – their flat flowerheads providing structure and layers of solid colour. They contrast dramatically with vertical flower spikes and soft, wispy grasses. They also thrive in poor, dry soils. 'Coronation Gold' is a dramatic plant, covered in hundreds of large yellow flowerheads. It flowered solidly for 19 weeks during our trial, giving a brilliant show. It was also one of the tallest varieties on trial, but generally didn't need staking. Deadhead flowers as they fade.

Height x spread: 85 x 100cm
Flowering period: May–October
`dry soil` :☀:
Also good for: Gravel gardens

Achillea 'Feuerland'

Most achillea flowers tend to fade by autumn, especially in hot weather, but this variety remained colourful late in the year during our trial. Flowers were blazing red with yellow centres when they appeared in mid-June (July in Scotland), becoming pale orange by September. All summer, plants were thick with blooms. Remarkably, despite reaching 80cm in height, 'Feuerland' didn't need staking at any of our test sites. Achilleas have aromatic leaves, which many people find unpleasant, so avoid planting them in large groups or where you will brush past them regularly. They can also aggravate skin conditions. Deadhead blooms regularly and divide in autumn or spring every three years.

Height x spread: 80 x 70cm
Flowering period: June–September
`dry soil` :☀:
Also good for: Gravel gardens

Eryngium x tripartitum

For bold blooms, consider *E.* x *tripartitum*. This flowers July–September, producing dramatic branching heads of purple-blue cones with grey bracts, standing 60cm tall. The best steely blue flowers are produced when it is grown in free-draining sandy soil. They have a wonderful metallic look, which is beautiful when grown en masse, especially in midsummer.

Height x spread: 60 x 30cm
Flowering period: July–September
dry soil :☀:
Also good for: Gravel gardens

> **Tip** Leave the old flower heads on eryngium as they look beautiful during winter when covered in frost. They can be cut to the ground when they eventually look too tatty.

Eryngium yuccifolium

E. yuccifolium looks rather like an elegant leek, with handsome glaucous leaves. For year-round interest, *E. yucciflorium* had good architectural foliage and flowers, and long-lasting seedheads. During our trial we were surprised to find they survived in Glasgow as they are reputed to be only partially hardy. Global warming may have its advantages! As an added safeguard in cold and exposed gardens, grow these in the middle to back of a sheltered border to give them protection and support from other plants. The grey flowers turn soft pink as they age.

Height x spread: 120 x 60cm
Flowering period: July–September
dry soil :☀:
Also good for: Foliage

Erigeron 'Dunkelste Aller'

This German-bred variety (also known as 'Darkest of All') was very floriferous even in the first year of our trial. Its upright stems bore clusters of 5-6cm-wide daisies that held up to wind without flinching. A great choice for cutting as well as the front of a sunny border, our eye-catching display lasted eight weeks on average. Not all of our plants bulked up as quickly as we'd have liked, so if you're buying small plants, consider investing in at least five to give a reasonable-sized clump from the outset.

Height x spread: 55 x 50cm
Flowering period: June–July
well-drained soil ☀
Also good for: Cutting

Erigeron glaucus 'Sea Breeze'

Unusually for an erigeron, this dwarf variety is evergreen and has a spreading habit. It was bred from a Californian wild flower called beach aster, found on sand dunes and cliffs, but overwintered well. Our trial sites enjoyed a generous display of 4cm-wide daisies for 10 weeks. The blooms are born on sturdy stems and are deep pink when they first open, but gradually fade to baby pink. Most plants benefited from a quick trim in spring. They are best planted in spring in a sunny, free-draining spot.

Height x spread: 30 x 60cm
Flowering period: June–August
`well-drained soil` ☀
Also good for: Ground cover

Erigeron karvinskianus

Also sold as 'Profusion', this dainty, drought-tolerant daisy is a Mexican native. It flowered from May until the first hard frosts with 2cm-wide flowers, and what they lack in size they make up for in quantity. They open white on wiry stems, age to dark pink and don't look a mess if not deadheaded. Unlike other erigeron, this one is easily raised from seed and is suitable for containers, borders and rockeries. Ours self-seeded at most sites.

Height x spread: 30 x 65cm
Flowering period: May–October
`well-drained soil` ☀
Also good for: Containers

Tip Deadheading erigerons can encourage a better show in late summer. Cut tall varieties to the ground after flowering. Trim low-growing types once they start looking tatty in winter or early spring.

Artemisia lactiflora (see page 134)

Plants
for foliage

It's all too easy to be seduced by colourful displays of flowers at the garden centre, but even the hardest working plants that bloom for months, can't compete with the length of time that foliage adds texture, shape and colour to the border.

Foliage brings so many qualities to a display. Perhaps the most obvious is colour. There are an amazing number of shades to choose from, including silver, gold, bronze, purple and, of course, green. Add to that the many plants that have variegation and you're spoilt for choice. Saying that, variegation is something that tends to divide opinion among gardeners between those who love it and those who can't bear it. If you're a little unsure, start with a subtle creamy edge or a gentle golden stripe, before progressing on to more strident combinations.

Leaf shape also plays a big part in the success of foliage in a planting scheme. Again there are lots of types to choose from, such as strappy leaves like phormium, round shapes, such as cotinus, and jagged edges, such as Japanese maples. Play around and find something that really sets off your display.

Finally, texture and even scent have a big part to play. Who can resist caressing soft leaves such as fur-covered stachys or a wispy grass? While the heady scents of many leaves, such as lavender and sage, are a real delight, especially on a warm day.

Foliage

Lavandula angustifolia 'Elizabeth'

Introduced by Downderry Nursery in 2007, this fantastic lavender is similar in colour to 'Hidcote', but slightly larger with bigger flower heads. During our trials, its mass of long, spreading flower spikes lasted slightly longer than those of 'Hidcote', too. When well looked after, lavender can live up to 20 years; French lavender less, at about 10 years. Plant them in a sunny site with well-drained soil; avoid planting under trees, and dig in plenty of grit on heavy soils or grow in a patio pot instead.

Height x spread: 60 x 80cm
Flowering period: June–August
`well-drained soil` ☀
Also good for: Scent, Bees and butterflies

Lavandula angustifolia 'Munstead'

In our tests, this old favourite lived up to expectations, with a cloud of lilac-blue flowers covering the compact plants. The scent was pleasant, though less noticeable compared with some varieties. Mulch with some well-rotted compost after planting, and water well until they are established. Don't add fertiliser as this tends to lead to unattractive leggy growth.

Height x spread: 50 x 65cm
Flowering period: June–July
`well-drained soil` ☀
Also good for: Scent, Bees and butterflies

Tip Pruning is vital to keep lavenders full of vigour. Prune in late summer when flowering is over. Trace the stems back to where they come out of the bush and cut off 2–5cm of leaf stalk, along with the stem.

Foeniculum vulgare 'Purpureum'

Leaf fennels are popular as much for their ornamental value as their aromatic leaves and seeds. Fairly trouble-free, 'Purpureaum' produces bronze-coloured clouds of evergreen, licorice-scented filigree foliage. The strong, zig-zag shaped stems open out into yellow umbels and, even though the foliage can start to yellow when the flowers finish, new leaves will soon be produced from the base to start the process over again. Fennels will happily self-seed over much of their surroundings and they look good planted with ornamental grasses.

Height x spread: 155 x 70cm
Flowering period: August–September
well-drained soil
Also good for: Scent

Artemisia pontica

A. pontica is a very good groundcover plant. It's a delicate plant, compact and aromatic with a faintly sweet smell. This useful plant will do well in full sun, even in poor soil. In our trial, the foliage stayed looking good for a long period over the growing season, but while it's usually evergreen, we found that in colder areas there won't be much to look at in the winter. Most artemisias are happiest in free-draining soils and cope well with drought. To keep them in shape, it's often necessary to cut them back by about a third or more for the very vigorous ones, in late May/early June, though most should also be cut down to the foliage at the base of the plant in autumn.

Height x spread: 55cm x indefinite spread
Flowering period: Not applicable
well-drained soil
Also good for: Gravel gardens

Artemisia lactiflora

This is an upright and self-supporting plant with a dark green jaggedly cut foliage. The graceful spires of white flowers lasted for about 11 weeks during our trial. The fresh green foliage at the base of the plant will remain over winter. Unusually for artemisia, this plant needs a moisture-retentive soil to do well – there were a few powdery mildew problems reported with this and the related 'Guizhou Group' during hot, dry spells.

Height x spread: 145 x 45cm
Flowering period: June–August
`moist soil` ☀
Also good for: Cottage garden border

Artemisia schmidtiana 'Nana'

This forms low mounds of small, silvery leaves described as 'tactile' by one assessor. Its cushion shape and soft foliage reminded another of a small, furry animal! To keep it in shape, it's best to remove the flower buds or chop it back by a third in early summer. Otherwise, it tends to open up in the middle and needs to be cut back to the new foliage at the base. Overall, it's a unique and very useful plant for the front of the border. Despite its reputation for being evergreen, at our trial sites it died down completely in winter. Try growing this variety with white dahlias and blue-leaved grasses.

Height x spread: 20 x 65cm
Flowering period: Not applicable
`well-drained soil` ☀
Also good for: Gravel gardens

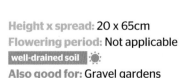

Geranium x monacense var. monacense 'Muldoon'

The interesting semi-evergreen foliage of 'Muldoon', with its distinctive purple patches on light-green leaves, made this geranium stand out in our borders during our trial. The purple staining on the leaves coordinated beautifully with the dark purple flowers, which were as popular with the bees as with our assessors. It's an early-flowering variety, and provides a good source of nectar for the bees in late spring. Fortunately for gardeners, hardy geraniums are virtually pest free, although they can occasionally suffer from rust and powdery mildew.

Height x spread: 45 x 60cm
Flowering period: May–June
well-drained, clay, acid and chalky soil
Also good for: Bees and butterflies

Astrantia major 'Sunningdale Variegated'

This astrantia has pinkish-white bracts above variegated leaves with white edges and patches of pale green that fade in summer. In bud, the colours of the Astrantia undersides of the bracts dominate. Then, as the tiny flowers are revealed, the inner surface of the bracts surrounding them conveys another tone. During our trial, *A. major* 'Sunningdale Variegated' put on a brilliant display of white-edged foliage in April, and again after flowering, even as late as November in our Glasgow site. The variegation faded almost to nothing by August, when it scorched slightly in north London in full sun, but otherwise fared well.

Height x spread: 90 x 45cm
Flowering period: June–September
moist soil
Also good for: Cottage garden border

Lathyrus odoratus 'Blue Shift' (see page 140)

Plants
for scent

Scent brings so much pleasure to gardening. Just a waft of a familiar perfume brings back instant memories of events, feelings and sights associated with it. There are so many plants that offer scents for us to enjoy, from either their flowers or their foliage.

Whether we can appreciate all of the scents on offer depends on the power of our sense of smell, which can vary a lot between individuals. Some days the scents can also be more elusive than others. The best days tend to be warm and still when perfumes hang in the air and you can catch wafts of them without having to stick your nose in to enjoy them.

There are also many different types of smell. Roses, for example, have a wide range of different scents depending on the variety, including fruity, myrrh and tea. Which you prefer varies between individuals,. You may feel that perfumes are heavenly, while others can stick in the throat. It's very much down to personal preference.

Many foliage plants need you to rub their leaves to release their scents, so make sure these are easily in reach so you can enjoy them. A lovely idea is to plant these species near a path where you will naturally brush them as you walk by.

Tulipa 'Dragon King'

'Dragon King' is a late-flowering tulip with long goblet-shaped flowers. Its exotic colouring gives it a rainbow effect, and its sumptuous multi-headed flowers have a distinct and delicious rose scent. In our trial, it grew and flowered well in both the bed and in a pot, where we mixed it with other pink tulips. It's a unique tulip and one that would create an interesting talking point in your garden.

Height: 35cm
Flowering period: April–May
 well-drained soil ☀
Also good for: Cut flowers

Narcissus 'Sweet Love'

During our trial, the first thing that struck us about this daffodil was the gorgeously sweet smell that infused the air around it; strong enough to attract our attention, but not overpowering. It stands proudly and the small flowers seem to shed the rain with ease. In our trial, there were many flower stems from each bulb that held two or more elegantly nodding, small-cupped flowers. Plant daffodils at two times the depth of the bulb. Not planting as deeply as this can lead to the bulbs failing to flower after the initial year.

Height: 30cm
Flowering period: April
well-drained soil ☀
Also good for: Cut flowers

Narcissus 'Lieke'

Our assessors really liked this daffodil. Its dainty flowers have an intriguing green eye and a lovely scent. It bloomed for 45 days, which is an eternity in daffodil terms. With three stems from each bulb and three flowers on each stem, there were plenty of blooms. They stayed upright despite the deluge of rain, and on lifting the bulbs we saw they had thrived. Don't be tempted to tie the foliage in knots to tidy up its appearance after flowering as this damages the leaves and reduces the amount of food they can make, which is vital for next year's display of flowers.

Height: 45cm
Flowering period: April–May
well-drained soil ☀
Also good for: Cut flowers

Tip To be sure of getting the exact varieties of spring bulbs that you want, it can be easier to buy them via mail order from a specialist bulb nursery.

Nemesia Lady Series

Nemesias are closely related to diascias and are a great choice for mixed plantings in pots. The Lady Series comprises three highly scented varieties. 'Sweet Lady' proved to be the longest flowering of the three and still looked good in September. It also had one of the most pleasing scents, with just enough perfume to turn heads without being overpowering. Mix slow-release fertiliser into the compost at planting time for the best displays. Towards the end of the season, feed with liquid tomato food to keep them going until the frosts.

Height x spread: 25 x 25cm
Flowering period: July–September
`well-drained soil` ☀
Also good for: Containers

Lathyrus odoratus 'Blue Shift'

In our trial, we were impressed by the two-tone colouring of its flowers, which first appear as red-purple and become blue with age. The flower stems were quite short (measuring about 13cm), so they weren't the best for cutting, but the scent was strong and very sweet. Our plants were producing copious quantities of flowers for about 10 weeks, until powdery mildew started to appear in August. We sowed our seeds in February, but sweet peas can also be sown in late October and overwintered in a sheltered spot. For the longest season of blooms, keep cutting them so they never have the chance to set seed.

Height x spread: 110 x 90cm
Flowering period: June–August
`well-drained soil` ☀
Also good for: Cut flowers

Lavandula angustifolia 'Hidcote'

This classic lavender showed us just why it remains so popular. It gave a long display of densely packed, deep purple flowers, with fantastic scent, over grey-blue leaves. If you want to enjoy the scent at other times of year, dry the flowers and put in cotton bags. They're great for freshening clothes in a drawer or even for infusing a bath with scent. Lavender is said to aid restful sleep.

Height x spread: 55 x 70cm
Flowering period: June–August
`well-drained soil` ☀
Also good for: Foliage, Bees and butterflies, Cut flowers

Gladiolus murielae

This gladiolus, often called acidanthera, not only looks lovely, but smells lovely, too; we found its sweet scent was noticeable from quite a distance. The plants have very long leaves and clusters of large, nodding white flowers with pretty markings on multiple stems. Ours didn't need staking and had a more delicate appearance than most of the other varieties we tested.

Height x spread: 90 x 30cm
Flowering period: August–September
`well-drained soil` ☀
Also good for: Gravel gardens

Tip Grow scented plants where you can easily access their flowers and foliage so you can enjoy them without having to clamber over other plants.

Echinacea 'Twilight'

This was one of the tallest and longest-flowering varieties in our trial. The thick fringe of petals started as a pretty shade of rose pink around an orange cone, fading to very pale pink. The petals stayed almost horizontal, and the flowers had a lovely sweet scent. The hairy dark green foliage grew almost to the top of the flowering stems, but the mass of flowers still managed to cover it. Plants needed some support when all the flowers were open – although they may have grown taller than usual over our two very wet summers.

Height x spread: 90 x 50cm
Flowering period: July–September
well-drained soil ☀
Also good for: Cottage garden border

Cosmos atrosanguineus 'Chocamocha'

Famous for its chocolate aroma, this variety didn't give off a strong smell at first in our trial, but by mid-August there was a definite 'Dairy Milk' scent near the blooms. Only a few flowers came out at any time to start with, so the visual impact wasn't striking until mid-August, when 'Chocamocha' would be great as a focal point in the middle or front of a border. The green leaves showed off the dark flowers well. This relatively small cosmos flowered longer than any other variety on trial – up to 17 weeks. 'Chocamocha' was the only perennial in our trial of cosmos and it can be grown from tubers, in the same way as dahlias.

Height x spread: 35 x 55cm
Flowering period: June–September
well-drained soil ☀
Also good for: Containers

Hemerocallis 'Frans Hals'

Each exotic day lily flower lasts for only a day but choose this variety and you won't go short – it produces up to 30 blooms on a single stem. It's a striking choice and would make a real splash in a 'hot' planting scheme – we think it would look good teamed with some red dahlias, for example. Keep it within sniffing distance, though, as it's one of the few day lilies with a strong, sweet scent. Hemerocallis sometimes produce baby plants on the flower stems. If you see them, pot them up and keep them protected until they start to grow and develop a root system the following year.

Height x spread: 100 x 120cm
Flowering period: July–September
`well-drained soil` ☀
Also good for: Cottage garden border

Antirrhinum majus 'Reminiscent'

This antirrhinum was easy to grow in our tests, coming into full flower in early July. It produced a mix of pastel-coloured flowers on short, compact plants. Once the plants had come into bloom, they continued to provide a good display right through to late September. The flowers had a distinct, citrus scent that's absent from most modern antirrhinum cultivars. Sow antirrhinum seeds in the greenhouse from January to March. It needs light to germinate, so don't cover. Prick into modular trays and plant out once the danger of frost has passed in late May or early June.

Height x spread: 25 x 25cm
Flowering period: July–September
`well-drained soil` ☀
Also good for: Containers

Petunia 'Sanguna Atomic Blue' (see page 153)

Plants
for containers

Whether you're planting up a window box, hanging basket or pot, the plants you choose need to be tough, colourful and long flowering. Every year there are plenty of new varieties in the garden centre and mail order catalogues so *Which? Gardening* grows as many as we can get our hands on and brings you best-performing varieties in a spring issue.

Make sure that the plants you buy are healthy. Check that they aren't root bound and carefully tease out the roots before planting.

Good compost can make a huge difference to your plants. We also release the results of our latest compost trials each year in a spring issue. You should also add a slow-release fertiliser to the compost before planting.

Use deep pots or baskets to improve root development and water retention. Use cone-shaped hanging baskets as they have extra depth.

Previous *Which? Gardening* research has shown that there is no need to add extra crocks to the bottom of pots to improve drainage. Just make sure the holes are large enough to allow excess water to easily drain away.

Water the compost, not the leaves, to avoid fungal problems. It's best to water plants thoroughly when needed rather than watering them little and often. Also, regularly remove dead or damaged flowers or foliage, and be vigilant for slugs, aphids or mildew. If blooms start to fade later in the season, give your pots a liquid feed.

Containers

Clematis 'Crystal Fountain'

In our trial, the large and remarkable double flowers were arranged in two layers, with the flat violet-blue petals below and paler quilled petals above. Our plants were bushy with a neat shape that they kept all season, making them ideal for pots. Blooms opened from the top to the bottom of the red stems, too, so we got a really good covering of flowers, and they managed three full flushes in one season. Use a large pot to give roots room to grow; roughly 45cm in diameter and depth, and use good-quality compost. If you use terracotta pots, line them with plastic before planting to reduce water loss in hot weather.

Height x spread: 150 x 70cm
Flowering period: May–June,
August, October
Also good for: Climber

Clematis 'The Vagabond'

The gorgeous cobalt blue of these very large flowers really stood out in our trial. Even when they faded to a more washed-out pinky blue, 'The Vagabond' still looked lovely. The sheer flower power was also outstanding: our plants were almost completely cloaked in vibrant blooms at their peak. Bushy plants, which didn't attempt a getaway, and silky, spidery seedheads also added to their charms. This is a fabulous plant from all angles.

Height x spread: 120 x 70cm
Flowering period: April–June
Also good for: Climber

Clematis 'Chantilly'

In our trials, we found that 'Chantilly' had large, blush-pink flowers that faded first to white with a pink stripe, and finally to pristine white. Rain didn't mark them, but they did turn brown once finished, so you might want to do some deadheading. Our plants also had a full, bushy shape and a good covering of flowers, which makes them ideal for growing in a pot. Prune in the spring to 30cm. Avoid clematis wilt (see Tip) by planting deeply so the top of the roots are below soil level. Add slow-release fertiliser when planting and in early spring each year. Topdress with compost annually.

Height x spread: 100 x 75cm
Flowering period: May–July
Also good for: Climber

Clematis 'Parisienne'

In our trial, this bushy variety produced masses of stems. We wrapped chicken wire around our second pot and easily trained the plants down it, in addition to climbing. The delicate violet shade of the large flowers, though not very unusual, looked pretty. There were masses of flowers and we got a second flush later in the summer.

Height x spread: 100 x 70cm
Flowering period: May–July
Also good for: Climber

Tip If clematis wilt does strike (plants suddenly develop black patches and wilt, usually just as they're about to flower), you'll need to cut back to ground level and destroy all affected growth. New shoots should grow from the roots.

Clematis 'Rebecca'

Described as 'divine' by one assessor, the huge, deep velvet-red flowers developed evenly all round our plants in a way that would make this variety a stunning focal point from any angle. The backs of the flowers were a pretty pink, and the lush, healthy growth filled out around the supports nicely. It also had attractive spidery seedheads and a second flush of flowers in August. Most varieties will grow better if you site them away from potential cold winds. Strong sun can fade flower colours. Move the pot so the plant gets some midday shade if necessary.

Height x spread: 110 x 75cm
Flowering period: May–June, August
☀ ◼
Also good for: Climber

Diascia 'Coral Belle'

Set against the cool green backdrop provided by our lime trees, the pale flowers of this diascia lit up. In our trial, they flowered brilliantly throughout the summer and were an overall favourite. They had smaller flowers and their growth was less dense than others, but this worked in their favour when they weaved their way through other plants in mixed baskets. If plants are set back by poor weather, or start to look messy as flowering slows, they can be easily tidied up by a quick trim with a pair of shears. Give them a liquid feed and they should start to flower again in a couple of weeks.

Height x spread: 20 x 35cm, trailing 5cm
Flowering period: June–October
☀
Also good for: Rockeries

Diascia Flying Colours Appleblossom

The best diascia we grew in our trial. The plants were quick to come into flower and produced copious amounts of very attractive, larger-than-average flowers all summer. The plants stayed very neat, initially growing quite upright, but then trailing as they got bigger. With no need to deadhead, they gave us a long-lasting and low-maintenance display. Diascias can be used in pots or baskets, but would be just as happy cascading down a rockery. As they come from drier climes, diascias don't need massive amounts of water; they don't like to have their feet wet and will benefit from good drainage.

Height x spread: 25 x 30cm, trailing 5cm
Flowering period: June–September
☀
Also good for: Rockeries

Osteospermum Serenity Series

Osteospermums are great for both patio pots and summer-bedding schemes. This series has delightful colours, with soft pastel or terracotta-toned flowers that mature to a deeper shade, giving a wonderfully warm appearance. Our plants filled our large pot, and though the dull summer meant they took a while to get going, by August they were in full force, only needing an occasional removal of any spent flowers. Try combining it with silver foliage such as *Helichrysum petiolare,* which will trail down the sides of the container.

Height x spread: 35 x 30cm
Flowering period: July–October
☀
Also good for: Gravel gardens

Petchoa
'SuperCal Vanilla Blush'

This hybrid is a cross between two garden favourites: petunia and calibrachoa. The mounded plants produced lots of medium petunia-like flowers, but, thanks to its calibrachoa heritage, unlike petunia flowers they weren't sticky, making deadheading a breeze. Our plants took a while to get established and benefited from feeding, but by mid-August they were really showing off their unusual creamy pink and yellow-tinted flowers. We found that 'SuperCal Vanilla Blush' did well in either a hanging basket or pot. Try planting it with purple osteospermums for a jazzy-looking mix.

Height x spread: 15 x 25cm
Flowering period: July–October
☀
Also good for: Summer flowers

Pelargonium Caliente Series

These perlargoniums are a cross between ivy-leaved types, renowned for their tough characteristics, and zonal types, which should give them extra flower power. Our plants flowered magnificently throughout the trial, the dark leaves complementing the bright blooms. They were very resilient, unaffected by anything the weather threw at them. Try taking cuttings in summer to have plants to overwinter indoors. Or, before the first frosts, cut back the main plant and bring it indoors to a light, frost-free place. Keep it on the dry side during winter and then increase watering in spring.

Height x spread: 35 x 40cm
Flowering period: June–October
☀
Also good for: Foliage

Verbena 'Lanai Pink Twister'

This eye-catching, two-tone verbena flowered prolifically in our trial. The plants didn't trail, but enjoyed spreading sideways, and as the weight of flowers increased they trailed further down the sides of the pot. As with most verbenas, they benefited from careful deadheading, which is essential to encourage the development of new buds. If you don't do this they'll come and go out of flower on a biweekly basis. When thinking what to combine it with, it either lends itself to a soft, romantic mix of pinks, silver and lavender or you could pick out the deeper pink of the flower buds and put it with something brighter.

Height x spread: 20 x 40cm, trailing to 15cm
Flowering period: July–October
☀
Also good for: Summer flowers

Calibrachoa 'Can-can Rose Star'

Calibrachoas have been subjected to a lot of new breeding to improve their performance, as previous strains have been choosy about soil types. This variety looks like a small-flowered petunia, and it formed nicely mounded plants that trailed well over the sides of the basket in our tests. These plants were almost faultless and they flowered much longer than many others. Give it ample water and extra feeding with tomato food to fuel its strong growth.

Height x spread: 20 x 30cm, trailing to 10cm
Flowering period: July–October
☀
Also good for: Summer flowers

Lobelia 'Super Star'

'Super Star' certainly lived up to its name – it was the best lobelia in our trial. This is a small-flowered, bicolour variety and our plants flowered prolifically, starting in June and continuing long after our other lobelias had given up entirely. They still looked fresh and bright in early October. However, unlike many lobelias, 'Super Star' isn't a trailing variety, and would therefore suit a pot better than a hanging basket. Make sure that you keep all lobelias well watered as they are susceptible to turning to straw if they get too dry. If this happens by accident to your plants, try cutting them to see if they regrow.

Height x spread: 20 x 25cm
Flowering period: July–September
☀ ▮
Also good for: Edging paths

Petunia 'Sanguna Atomic Blue'

'Atomic Blue' is an apt name for this petunia; the flowers have a dark throat and dark veins that lead into the deep-mauve colour of the rounded petals. It was a great performer in our trial and carried on flowering when many others were waning. Our plants trailed well and didn't suffer, as some petunias do, from having all the flowers at the bottom of a curtain of green growth. Petunias work best when they are planted without other types of plant as they will easily fill a hanging basket or patio container with colour.

Height x spread: 15 x 30cm, trailing to 20cm
Flowering period: July–October
☀
Also good for: Summer flowers

Petunia 'Pretty Much Picasso'

You will either love or loathe the flamboyant pink flowers of this aptly named petunia. Our plants were prolific: just two managed to fill, cover and trail from our basket, and they flowered non-stop for most of the trial. They required very little deadheading to keep them looking good and only started to look a bit bedraggled in late October, when powdery mildew took its toll on all the petunias in our trial. Heavy rain can knock back petunias and leave the flowers looking rather soggy, but don't worry as they'll soon bounce back once the weather improves.

Height x spread: 25 x 40cm
Flowering period: June–September
☀
Also good for: Summer flowers

Bidens 'Solaire Semidouble'

This well-behaved variety of bidens is excellent for mixed plantings in pots or hanging baskets. It forms a dense trailing mat of fine foliage, covered with hundreds of tiny, vibrant flowers that have an extra set of petals around the eye, forming a frilly collar. Our plants grew well and flowered strongly all summer. They did benefit from deadheading, but this was a simple task as the spent flowers were easy to spot and pick off. Try planting it with blue flowers for an eye-catching display.

Height x spread: 15 x 30cm, trailing to 15cm
Flowering period: June–September
☀
Also good for: Foliage

Sunpatiens Compact Series

We found these New Guinea-type impatiens to be extremely vigorous, with remarkable flowering performance. They are tolerant of both sun and shade, and shouldn't succumb to the dreaded downy mildew, which can devastate busy lizzies. The lovely dark leaves and vibrant flowers only required a little tidying to stay looking pristine. Impatiens downy mildew causes ordinary impatiens to show patches of furry mould on the underside of leaves, which then yellow and drop, causing the death of the plants. Fortunately sunpatiens seem to be resistant. They are thirsty plants, but keep them well hydrated and they will impress you with their consistent, trouble-free flowering.

Height x spread: 45 x 40cm
Flowering period: July–October
☀◐■
Also good for: Foliage

Agapanthus 'Peter Pan'

This is a compact evergreen agapanthus with sparser flower heads than many varieties, but lots of flower stems shot up in our trial, which gave plenty of impact. This variety's neat shape would suit the front of a border or a container. Lift and divide the plant every couple of years to avoid it getting congested as they don't like to be potbound, as they become hard to water.

Height x spread: 50 x 60cm
Flowering period: July–August
☀
Also good for: Gravel gardens

Other Which? Books

Which? Books provide impartial, expert advice and easy-to-follow tutorials covering subjects from gardening and computing to finance, property and major life events. We also publish the country's most trusted restaurant guide, The Good Food Guide. To find out more about Which? Books, log on to **www.which.co.uk/books** or call **01992 822800**.

Growing Your Own Vegetables Made Easy
ISBN: 978 1 84490 128 9
Price: £10.99
From carrots to courgettes, learn how to cultivate your favourite produce with *Growing Your Own Vegetables Made Easy*. Compiled by the *Which? Gardening* experts, the book shows you how to sow, grow and harvest a wide range of vegetables, and also features advice on preventing and controlling pests and diseases.

The Gardener's Year Made Easy
ISBN: 978 1 84490 120 3
Price: £10.99
Whether you want to care for your borders or tend your vegetable plot, *The Gardener's Year Made Easy* guides you through the essential garden tasks month by month. Showing you what to do and when, this practical handbook sets out the tasks to complete each month to keep your garden in tip top shape. The book includes advice on lawns, borders, fruit and vegetables as well as the pests and diseases to look out for.

Tracing Your Family History Made Easy
(includes CD-Rom)
ISBN: 978 1 84490 124 1
Price: £12.99
Researching your family tree is a fascinating and fulfilling project, but where do you begin? This handy book will show you how, with step-by-step instructions and tips guide you through the entire process, from searching historical records to locating online resources. Understand how to check census records, interpret documents and learn how to build your family tree on your home computer.

About Which?

Which? is the largest independent consumer body in the UK. A not-for-profit organisation, we exist to make individuals as powerful as the organisations they deal with in everyday life. Our campaigns make people's lives fairer, simpler and safer. This page gives you a taster of some of our many products and services.

Which? Online and Which? Local

www.which.co.uk is updated regularly, so you can read hundreds of product reports and Best Buy recommendations, keep up to date with Which? campaigns, compare products, use our financial planning tools and search for the best cars on the market. As a Which? member you can sign up to Which? Local, a website of 110,000 local business reviews created for Which? members, by Which? members. Covering everything from plumbers to plasterers and butchers to bakers, our independent member reviews will help you find the best service that won't charge you over the odds. To subscribe, go to www.which.co.uk.

Which? Legal Service

Which? Legal Service offers convenient access to first-class legal advice at unrivalled value. One low-cost annual subscription enables members to receive tailor-made legal advice by telephone or email on a wide variety of legal topics,

For more information, log onto www.which.co.uk or call 01992 822800.

including consumer law – problems with goods and services, employment law (for employees), holiday problems, neighbour disputes, parking tickets and Wills and Probate Administration in England and Wales. To subscribe, call the Members' helpline: 01992 822828 or go to www.whichlegalservice.co.uk.

Which? Money

Whether you want to boost your pension, make your savings work harder or simply need to find the best credit card, Which? Money has the information you need. Which? Money offers you honest, unbiased reviews of the best (and worst) personal finance deals, from bank accounts to loans, credit cards to savings accounts. It's also packed with investigations, revealing the truth behind the small print. As a Which? member you also have access to the Which? Money helpline offering free one-to-one guidance on any financial matter. To subscribe, go to www.which.co.uk/money-subscription.

Picture credits

Picture credits

Key: T = top picture, B = bottom picture

All pictures courtesy of *Which? Gardening*: Jonathan Buckley: pages 25 T, 29 T, 29 B, 30, 31 T, 31 B, 37 B, 96 T, 96 B, 97 T, 103 T, 103 B, 120 B, 148 B, 149 **Sarah Cuttle:** pages 18 T, 18 B, 19 T, 19 B, 24 T, 24 B, 28 T, 28 B, 33 T, 33 B, 34, 41 B, 42 T, 42 B, 43 T, 46 T, 46 B, 47 T, 50 B, 57 B, 62, 63 T, 63 B, 65 T, 65 B, 70, 75 T, 75 B, 84, 89 T, 89 B, 100 T, 100 B, 101 T, 102 T, 102 B, 110 T, 111 B, 113, 114, 118 T, 118 B, 119 T, 119 B, 121, 123 T, 123 B, 132 T, 132 B, 136, 140 T, 140 B, 141 T, 143 B, 144, 150 T, 150 B, 151 T, 151 B, 152 T, 152 B, 153 T, 153 B, 154 T, 154 B, 155 **Paul Debois:** pages 25 B, 68 T, 77 T, 97 B, 110 B, 112 T, 112 B, 120 T, 146 T, 146 B, 147 T, 147 B, 148 T **John Glover:** page 86 B **Annaïck Guitteny:** pages 7, 8, 11 T, 12 B, 14 T, 14 B, 38, 39 T, 39 B, 40 T, 47 B, 49 B, 67, 92, 98 T, 98 B, 108, 138, 139 T, 139 B, 141 B **Lynne Mack:** pages 54 T, 54 B, 83 T **Howard Rice:** pages 17 T, 17 B, 20, 23 T, 23 B, 32 T, 32 B, 44, 49 T, 51, 56, 60, 64 T, 66 T, 66 B, 68 B, 69 T, 69 B, 74 T, 74 B, 78, 82 T, 82 B, 86 T, 87 B, 88, 90 T, 90 B, 91, 95 B, 101 B, 122, 124, 126 T, 126 B, 128, 129 T, 129 B, 130, 133 B, 134 T, 134 B, 142 T, 143 T **Howard Rice / Mark Scott:** Page 83 B Freia Turland: pages 4, 52, 57 T, 133 T, 142 B **Rachel Warne:** pages 10, 11 B, 12 T, 13, 16, 22, 27, 36 T, 36 B, 37 T, 64 T, 94, 95 T, 104 T, 104 B, 105, 106, 109 T, 109 B, 111 T, 116, 117 T, 117 B

With the exception of the following pictures, which are published courtesy of: **Alamy:** pages 15 T © Science Photo Library / Alamy, 15 B © Martin Hughes-Jones / Alamy, 26 T © Dave Bevan / Alamy, 26 B © Christopher Burrows / Alamy, 40 B © Martin Hughes-Jones / Alamy, 41 T © Christopher Burrows / Alamy, 50 T © MBP-one / Alamy, 55 B © Andrea Jones / Alamy, 58 T © Martin Hughes-Jones / Alamy, 58 B © John Martin / Alamy, 59 B © John Martin / Alamy, 73 B © John Glover / Alamy, 76 B © Steffen Hauser / botanikfoto / Alamy, 77 B © John Glover / Alamy, 80 T © Ros Drinkwater / Alamy, 80 B © John Glover / Alamy, 81 T © Holmes Garden Photos / Alamy, 81 B © Factoryhill / Alamy, 87 T © Martin Hughes-Jones / Alamy, 99 T © Martin Hughes-Jones / Alamy, 99 B © John Glover / Alamy, 127 T © Holmes Garden Photos / Alamy, 127 B © Martin Hughes-Jones / Alamy, 135 T © Martin Hughes-Jones / Alamy, 135 B © Holmes Garden Photos / Alamy **Garden World Images:** page 43 B © MAP/ Nathalie Pasquel **Shutterstock:** pages 59 T © Jonathan Stokes / Shutterstock, 73 T © Laborant / Shutterstock, 76 T © Lijuan Guo / Shutterstock **Superstock:** pages 48 © Marka / SuperStock, 55 T © Gardenpix / SuperStock , 72 © age fotostock / SuperStock